Little Helpers
Toddler Baking
Cookbook

Little Helpers

Toddler Baking Cookbook

SWEET AND SAVORY RECIPES
TO MAKE, BAKE, AND SHARE

Barbara Lamperti

PHOTOGRAPHY BY LAURA FLIPPEN

ROCKRIDGE
PRESS

Interior and Cover Designer: Regina Stadnik
Art Producer: Tom Hood
Editors: Anne Lowrey and Ada Fung
Production Editor: Nora Milman

Photography and styling by Laura Flippen © 2021

ISBN: Print 978-1-64876-070-9 | eBook 978-1-64876-071-6
R0

To the boys in my life:
Albert, Luca, and Alex.
You are my everything.

contents

Introduction—CIAO!

"Mamma, what are you making? Can I help?" That glimpse of excitement in my little one's eyes; that quick run to the kitchen closet to grab his little folding step stool—those moments will always melt my heart and make me feel happy and proud. Cooking with kids gives back to us in so many ways.

My very first memory of my kids engaging with the kitchen world is their little fingers pushing the food processor button: on/off, on/off, on/off. Their surprised faces staring at the ingredients blending together, changing color, and transforming into a smooth purée, their little hands covering their ears to mute the loud sound of the machine—what an exciting adventure!

My children were toddlers when we started cooking together. We learned how to bake cookies first; an easy recipe, almost impossible to fail. If you're thinking about introducing your little one to the pleasure of cooking, I suggest starting with baking. A baking recipe has easy steps: measure, mix, stir, combine, bake. There is very little cutting, chopping, or stovetop cooking involved—no knives or flames to worry about!

Baking activates all the senses: kneading dough, smelling spices, watching the ingredients come together, listening to the crack of the egg and the electric beater, and, of course, tasting the final result. Sensory play is a huge part of a child's physical and cognitive growth. The simple action of rolling out dough with a rolling pin helps improve motor skills. Pouring milk into a bowl or filling a muffin tin with batter builds your little one's hand-eye coordination.

Baking also has emotional benefits. Focusing on the baking process is a calming activity for kids. The fact that there is a reward at the end that you can enjoy together makes everything more fun!

Baking together also helps with picky eating. Participating in the process and being able to touch, smell, and play with an ingredient makes it more familiar, and consequently more trustworthy and worth a try.

Yes, baking with little ones can be messy. They can lose their focus and you can lose your patience. But you will cherish the benefits and the memories. A little one's giggle is worth some flour on the floor and muffin batter on the fridge. In addition to recipes and tips, I hope this book will give you the reassurance that baking together will pay off in many ways. Get ready with your aprons, whisk, and spatulas for a fun and relaxed baking session with your little helpers—and don't forget to take pictures!

Happy Baking!

HOW TO USE THIS BOOK

You'll find five chapters in this book. The first chapter is an introduction to baking with toddlers. I share tips, tricks, suggestions, shortcuts, and strategies to help you prep and plan a fun baking session, some basic baking techniques, and a few safety guidelines. I've also listed some recommended tools and ingredients to have on hand so you're always ready to bake. The next four chapters are dedicated to the recipes, grouped by baking category: cakes, scones, and muffins; bread, biscuits, and pizza; cookies, crackers, and bars; and pies and pastries. I've included a variety of both sweet and savory recipes. You will see that the sweet recipes are not overly sweet but definitely flavorful. Maple syrup is the preferred added sweetener and used in moderation. I also aim to expose kids to delicious baked savory treats, even some filled with vegetables. Sweet or savory, every recipe is a nice treat, yummy and appealing to little ones, with a good balance of flavor and nutrition.

Recipe Levels: You will find three levels of difficulty indicated, with level 1 being the easiest. That said, all the recipes have been selected keeping in mind that you are baking with a toddler. There is no master chef level here! Here are the levels in more detail:

Level 1: Perfect for beginners or young toddlers. You might want to start with these recipes if it's the first time you're baking with your little one, if their attention span is limited, if they're still working on beginning motor skills or hand-eye coordination, or if you don't have a lot of time. Level 1 recipes are not long, and all the prep (measuring

and chopping) is done by the adult. Your little helper can get involved once all the tools and measured ingredients are lined up on the working table and the oven is preheating. They will engage in pouring, mixing, combining, and mashing.

Level 2: Great for toddlers who have already tried cooking and whose attention span is a bit longer. They can help you prepare and measure ingredients. They'll also get the chance to whisk, roll, knead, and shape dough. Even so, these recipes have an easy sequence of steps and don't require a lot of time.

Level 3: For more confident toddlers or younger kids. All the prep work can be done by your little helper under your supervision, and many steps can be done independently. These recipes might require some stovetop cooking or longer waiting times.

Recipe Labels: The following dietary labels will be added to recipes, if applicable: Dairy-Free, Egg-Free, Gluten-Free, Nut-Free, and Vegetarian or Vegan. Keep an eye out if allergies are a concern.

Recipe Method: Each step is color-coded, distinguishing steps that kids can likely do from those that adults should take the lead on. However, you know your child best and should judge for yourself what parts of the recipe they are best suited to do. Recipe instructions are color-coded as follows:

 Steps for Kids   ② **Steps for Adults**

Every recipe is accompanied by a tip. These include:

Baker's Tip: These tips provide extra details about the recipe or shortcuts you can use for a better result, such as chilling, freezing, cooling-down tricks, reasons to use a specific pan, or what to do with leftovers.

Heads Up: Some recipes might have a step that requires a bit more attention. These tips will alert you and give you an alternative or easy fix.

Make It Fun!: These tips will give you more ideas to make baking together even more playful, and are great for when you have some extra time. For example, number cookie cutters can transform a baking session into a number game.

Mix It Up: This is one of my favorite sections! I'll show you two different variations of the main recipe with a few easy substitutions. You may like a sweet recipe, but you would like to try the savory alternative. Or your toddler loves the main recipe, and the alternative has a new ingredient you want them to try. Swapping ingredients, shapes, and methods, as well as reinventing leftovers, teaches your little helper to think outside the box.

Recipe Notes: Here's where you will transform my cookbook into a personalized keepsake. Write down with your toddler when you baked the recipe, what you enjoyed the most, how many stars you'd rate it, and the best part—any funny anecdote that happened. Just imagine finding this cookbook in a box 20 years from now and reading this section. So many happy memories will resurface; you might even want to bake again together with your adult child—this time with no different steps for adults and kids!

LET'S GET STARTED!

Let's Bake

You and your little ones are probably very excited and ready to bake something yummy together! But before you jump into the recipes, I recommend taking a few minutes to read this chapter. As you well know, a toddler's attention span is *short*. That's why planning ahead is essential. I'll share some advice to make baking with your little one as fun and stress-free as possible. So, let's put our whisk down for a minute and talk about the ingredients and tools you'll need for the recipes in this book, the baking concepts you can teach, and, of course, a few safety rules.

MIX AND KNEAD, PLAY AND LEARN

I still remember baking with my grandmother in Italy. I recall feeling the cookie dough between my fingers; the sweet, warm scents wafting from the oven; the giant rolling pin that was so much fun to play with; and eating the best cookies ever. These warm and fuzzy feelings are one reason I bake with my two kids. Here are a few others:

Baking together helps you bond and build memories for a lifetime. My little nieces live on the other side of the world, and although I only see them once a year, we find time to bake together on our visits. It's my way of sharing my passion with them and a fun time for us to catch up and share family stories. Every time you and your child bake together is a special time for having fun, with minimal distractions from everyday life.

Kids who help in the kitchen are more willing to try new foods. When kids are involved in preparing food, they get excited about what they will eat at the end because it's "their" creation. But even if they don't end up trying the dish or eating very much of it, don't feel discouraged, because you've increased their exposure to a new food. Keep getting them involved—they might try it next time!

Baking enhances fine motor skills. Baking is full of opportunities to develop fine motor skills. Whether it's kneading dough, tracing straight lines while cutting crackers, or pouring liquids into a bowl, baking helps your little one's development.

Baking is a projects-based class. Kids can practice their numbers by counting out the berries they use to decorate a cake. They learn new words. Every word you use and demonstrate—blend, crimp, drizzle, dust—will enrich and expand their world. They can even see science in action as they watch butter melt in the microwave or marvel at pizza dough that's doubled in size.

Baking is easier than cooking. Common baking skills, like mixing, kneading, and decorating, are very toddler-friendly. There is little to no knife use and stovetop time in these recipes. All the knife prep and stovetop cooking are done by adults, and much of it can be done before you invite your little helper in.

Don't be afraid that your little one might be too young to start. This book's recipes were developed with two- to four-year-olds in mind; that's when I started baking with my boys and nieces. Remember that every recipe is split into "kid" steps and "adult" steps, so feel free to adapt the recipe instructions to suit your little helper's abilities and attention span.

WHY BAKE WITH PICKY EATERS?

My blog, *BuonaPappa,* was born thanks to my own picky eater. I tried many different strategies to get my kid to try new foods, and to avoid mealtime power struggles. What I found most successful (and enjoyable!) was to get my picky eater involved in cooking. Exposure is key here: The more pressure-free interactions your little one has with food—looking, smelling, touching, mixing, taste-testing—the more comfortable they will feel trying it. Inviting your child to help out in the kitchen also gives them a sense of control.

Baking together might be the best way to start. Think about it: In a toddler's mind, baking has many positive associations. Baked goods are soft, fluffy, and have reassuring smells and calming colors. Baked goods are also typically associated with celebrations—birthdays, parties, special occasions—it's no wonder they are so popular! Toddlers already know what cookies, bread, pizza, and muffins are, and that makes them great vehicles for getting them to try unfamiliar ingredients that may accompany these foods.

I'm a mom, so I have to say it: Safety is the most important ingredient for a perfect bake. Talk about kitchen safety with your little ones before you even preheat the oven. You can make it fun—my kids and I like playing the "safety rules quiz" with edible prizes like fruit, chocolate chips, and cheese cubes. After all, we want baked goods, not boo-boos!

General Kitchen Safety

Prepare the kitchen before you start. Kitchens are full of fascinating, potentially dangerous tools and appliances. Before you invite your little helper in, quickly scan the room to make sure everything is safe and clean. Make sure scissors and knives are out of reach, cabinets and drawers are closed, and, if possible, the sink is empty. If the recipe requires a food processor or mixer, place it on the work surface unplugged but ready to use. Clear a space for you and your toddler to work. Set out a kitchen helper tower or step stool so your little one can safely reach the work surface. Bonus—a tidy kitchen and well-appointed workspace will help your toddler focus more and increase your chances of finishing the recipe without too many distractions.

Always have a baking buddy. "I can do it myself." We've all heard our toddlers say that! There are tasks your little one can handle on their own, like stirring batter or sprinkling on toppings. I even encourage you to let them take the reins a bit—it'll help develop their self-esteem and independence. But remind your little one that you're their "baking buddy"—some tasks will be "grown-ups only" and others you can share and take turns.

Wash your hands. This can be fun—after all, there's bubbly soap and water involved! Remind your toddler that they need to wash their hands before starting, after cracking eggs or kneading dough, and whenever their hands are dirty or sticky with food.

Clean as you go, and clean when you're done. This rule can prevent spills and slips! Have your little helper assist in wiping up any spills as you go—remind them that keeping a tidy surface is important for food safety. And once you're done baking, have them help you double-check that the oven is off and appliances are unplugged.

Working with Raw Eggs

Raw eggs can contain salmonella that can give adults food poisoning, and it's even more dangerous for little ones. Gently explain to your toddlers that eating raw eggs will make their tummy hurt, which is why it's important to wash hands after handling raw eggs and to ask before taste-testing any food. Offer them a little bowl of something to snack on as an alternative, like chocolate chips, fruit, nuts, or other mix-ins and toppings you might already be prepping for the recipe.

To avoid cross-contamination, crack any eggs with your little ones before starting a recipe, away from the other ingredients. This way, you can clean up any accidents, wash hands, and have the eggs safely contained and ready to be added to the recipe.

Oven Safety

I don't mind that my kids are just a little bit scared of the oven—respectfully scared, that is! Gently guide your little one's hands safely near the preheating oven, just close enough to feel a little bit of the heat. Explain that the oven can get very hot like lava, so they should stand away from it and not touch it while it's on. Kids are naturally curious and will want to watch their creations bake. If your oven has a light, they can peek without getting too close.

Although your little helper likely won't be operating the oven, they'll start to learn good oven practices by watching you safely opening and closing the door, keeping your body at a distance, and always wearing dry oven mitts.

WHAT ABOUT KNIVES?

Luckily, baking doesn't require a lot of cutting or chopping. But baking can be a good starting point for teaching your toddler how to handle knives, such as with a butter knife or nylon kid's knife (easily purchased online) and a soft fruit like bananas or strawberries. Show them that the thinner side is the sharp edge—it does all the work. Show them how to hold the knife, and position the hand holding the food in a claw shape so little fingers are tucked away and never go beyond the blade of the knife. Explain that you use a cutting board and never cut in your hand. Even if you don't have your little ones help with slicing, you can show them how you use it and talk them through the correct hand position and movements.

In this section, I'll provide a quick list of tools, bakeware, and ingredients you'll want to have, so you're all set up to bake with your little one!

Setups for Your Little Helper

Tower or step stool. One of the most useful purchases I've made is a kitchen helper tower (a sturdy step stool will work, too). Those extra inches will allow toddlers to easily reach the countertop and be part of the action. It should be sturdy, easy to clean, and easy to move and store.

Kids' corner. If you have the space, I recommend creating a "kids' corner" with a small table and chairs, where little ones can sit and help or keep themselves busy with other activities while you cook.

Their own kitchen drawer. You may want to dedicate a lower cabinet or drawer to toddler-safe kitchen tools to play with. I had one for my boys when they were young, filled with plastic containers with lids, kids' aprons, spatulas, and a silicone collapsible strainer that served as a funny hat and melted my heart every time. Throw in a spare set of unbreakable measuring cups and spoons, so they can use "their set" to help you bake!

Tools and Appliances

Cooling racks. Racks help baked goods cool down faster and more evenly. Use one to glaze a cake; the extra glaze can simply drip through the rack instead of pooling around your cake and making the bottom soggy.

Electric hand mixer or stand mixer. Electric hand mixers are cheaper and can do most of what a stand mixer can. If you make a lot of bread, you might want to invest in a stand mixer to make easy work of kneading dough.

Food processor or blender. Great for chopping nuts, oats, or blending together ingredients.

Parchment paper or silicone mat. Useful for almost every baking recipe, these tools will save you so much cleanup time.

Prep and mixing bowls. You'll need a few bowls in various sizes, including a couple of medium to large ones for mixing batters and doughs. I also like to premeasure ingredients into little bowls before inviting my little helpers in. Stainless steel and bamboo bowls are great, because they're lightweight and almost impossible to break.

Rolling pin. Rolling, mashing, pressing—these are all fun activities for little ones to do with a rolling pin! I like to have two: one for me and one for my little helper.

Spatula. You can never have enough spatulas! I love having a variety in different colors and sizes, all made from versatile, heat-resistant silicone. But you can get by with just two or three.

Wet and dry measuring cups and spoons. If you give your child their own set, look for a lightweight and nonbreakable material like stainless steel, silicone, or plastic.

Whisk. This is great for blending together ingredients. A whisk is much easier than an electric hand mixer for little ones to manage. I prefer a stainless steel one, because it's easier to clean.

Wooden spoon. Great for scooping and mixing, because it is bigger and sturdier than a regular spoon.

Zester. I find this is easier and safer for little hands than a grater. Great for zesting citrus and finely grating Parmesan and chocolate.

Bakeware

9-inch round cake pan. Either a regular or springform nonstick pan will work for your cake needs.

9-by-5-inch loaf pan. Perfect for breads, pound cakes, and banana breads. I like these in nonstick carbon steel or silicone.

9-by-13-inch rectangular and 8-inch square pans. Great for brownies, bars, or any other baked goods that will be cut into squares. I like nonstick, ceramic, or glass.

11-inch tart pan. For tarts, pies, crostatas, and quiches. I find nonstick ones with removable bottoms the easiest to use.

12-cup muffin tins. Great for muffins and cupcakes. I like nonstick carbon steel or silicone.

Half-sheet baking pans (large baking sheets). Perfect for baking cookies, pizza, focaccia, scones, and biscuits. It's the bakeware piece I use the most. I prefer stainless steel ones, but aluminum will work fine.

Fun Extras

Cookie cutters. Sure, you can cut out circles with the rim of a glass, but cookie cutters make everything more fun! There is a wide world of fun cutters out there, including shapes, numbers, letters, seasonal themes, animals—the list goes on.

Ice-cream or cookie scoops. Use these tools to get evenly sized cookies or fill muffin tins with batter.

Liners. Muffins and cupcakes are more fun with a seasonal paper liner or colorful silicone liner.

Piping bags. A plastic bag with a corner cut off will allow you to make simple frosted decorations. If you want to upgrade to more detailed decorations, you can get a set of piping bags and tips.

Specialty baking pans and sheets. You might want to purchase additional bakeware to expand the kinds of baked goods you can make. A few to consider include mini and jumbo muffin tins, a round pizza sheet pan with holes, mini round cake pans for toddler-size cakes, and Bundt and ring cake pans.

Ingredient Staples

The core ingredients for baking are easy to find at most grocery stores. You'll want to keep the following ingredients stocked at home, so you're always ready to bake.

Baking powder and baking soda. Baking soda and baking powder are chemical leaveners. They differ in how they are activated and baking soda is much stronger, but they both lighten and aerate baked goods.

Cheese. Parmesan is a very kid-friendly cheese. It has a lovely flavor and melts well. I like to keep cheddar on hand as well.

Dried, fresh, and frozen fruits. Fruit is perfect for adding natural sweetness to your baked goods. I like to have bananas, apples, and berries (fresh or frozen) on hand. Dried fruit like apricots, cranberries, and dates are great, too.

Dye-free sprinkles. Some countries have banned food dyes. I prefer to avoid food dyes, and I buy dye-free sprinkles (available at Whole Foods and online). Additionally, I think if kids get used to enjoying sweets colored the way nature intended, it will be easier for them to enjoy other natural-color foods.

Eggs. In this book, I use medium eggs; either white or brown. If possible, I recommend organic eggs.

Extra-virgin olive oil. My favorite oil for any savory recipe.

Flour. It's the main ingredient for almost every recipe in this book. For sweet recipes, I use all-purpose unbleached flour or all-purpose whole-wheat flour—either one will work. For bread recipes, I suggest using a bread flour. It has more gluten and protein to give stretch and elasticity to your dough. Bread flour also comes in unbleached and whole-wheat varieties. If you have room for just one flour in your kitchen, all-purpose flour will do the job.

Herbs and spices. Good basic spices for sweet recipes are cinnamon and nutmeg. For savory recipes, oregano, thyme, and marjoram are my winning trio.

Instant active yeast or active dry yeast. Yeast comes in small packets and has the form of tiny brownish grains. It's essential for bread and pizza recipes.

Milk and yogurt. I typically use full-fat organic cow's milk and plain organic Greek yogurt in my recipes. You can substitute almond or coconut milk and yogurt for a dairy-free option, or a lactose-free milk if you want to avoid lactose.

Rolled oats. Good for breakfast *and* for baking!

Semisweet chocolate chips. These are a must for baking with kids! I like semisweet chocolate because it is not overly sweet.

Sweeteners. I mainly use maple syrup and some granulated cane sugar as needed for structure in my recipes. Honey will work as a substitute for maple syrup, but don't feed honey to a baby younger than one year old. Granulated coconut sugar can substitute for cane sugar.

Unrefined coconut oil. I like to use this in some sweet recipes instead of butter, for the background coconut flavor.

Unsalted butter. I find the 16-ounce box with four individual sticks very useful for measurements.

Unsweetened cocoa powder. Because we all love brownies!

Vanilla extract. Vanilla comes in a wide range of quality. I strongly suggest getting a pure vanilla extract, as opposed to a "vanilla-flavored" option. You won't need a huge quantity, and one bottle will last you a long time. The investment is totally worth it in terms of flavor.

SUGAR AS A SOMETIMES FOOD

Can my kids have sugar? How much is too much? Which kind of sugar is best? Sugar is a tricky and hotly debated topic among parents. Of course, our kids' health is a priority, and a diet with too much sugar can, in the long-term, cause diabetes, obesity, cardiovascular disease, and gum and tooth decay. Conversely, limiting sugar too much can put it on a pedestal and lead to sugar cravings, where kiddos might feel the need to "sneak" sugar when you're not around.

The American Heart Association, supported by the American Association of Pediatrics, recommends that toddlers under 2 years of age should avoid any added sugar in their diet, and that kids aged 2 to 18 should not consume more than 6 teaspoons of added sugar per day. It's important to understand what these organizations mean by "added" sugar. Many foods contain natural sugars, including vegetables, fruit, and animal

milks. Added sugars are sweeteners that are added to your food; these are the sugars we should try to limit in our kids' diets.

Moderation is key. A bit of added sugar now and then won't hurt, and making your own baked goods is a good way to know how much your kiddo is eating. I try to use added sugars that still have some nutrients, such as maple syrup. Also, honey is a complete food with medicinal properties. It bears repeating that honey should not be offered to babies under one year old to avoid possible botulism poisoning. For granulated sugar, natural cane sugar or coconut sugar are good choices.

The sweet recipes in this book rely more on moderate amounts of natural sweeteners to please your little one's sweet tooth. You will also find many savory recipes here. A mix of savory and sweet baked goods and thoughtful use of added sugars helps create a good balance for kids and prevent intense cravings.

TEACHING BAKING SKILLS

Baking is an art and a science, but it's not rocket science! Anyone can learn to bake and enjoy the results. In this section, you'll find advice and tips for how to teach your toddler the most foundational baking skills.

How to Crack an Egg

Cracking eggs is fascinating to little ones, but I get why it's an area of stress for adults! I suggest cracking the eggs into a separate bowl first. That way, you can fish out any broken eggshells.

1. Hold the egg and tap it flat against the base of the bowl or a clean, flat surface until you hear a crack.

2. Holding the egg over the bowl with both hands, gently press your thumbs into the crack, and pull the shell apart into two halves.

3. Let the egg fall into the bowl and keep the shell in your hands. *You did it— now let's wash up!*

How to Measure

Measuring ingredients carefully and precisely is an essential part of baking prep. Depending on the age and stage of your little one, you might decide to measure everything out ahead of time. If you want to involve them, here are some tips:

- When measuring dry ingredients like flour and sugar from a big bag or container, use a tablespoon to slowly fill the cup over the container—this will be much less messy than putting the cup right into the container.

- Show your kiddo how to swipe a clean finger or butter knife across the top to level it. Have them do it over the container to avoid spills.

- When measuring liquids, ask your child to bend down so they are at eye level with the measuring cup. Show them which mark you need to reach, and ask them to tell you when you've reached it as you pour.

- When measuring sticky ingredients like nut butters, grease your measuring tool with a bit of oil to help it easily slide into the bowl.

How to Pour

Pouring liquids without spilling can be challenging for little ones. Here are some tips for teaching your little one to pour:

- Use cups with handles. It's easier for your little one to pour a liquid from a measuring cup or smaller container with a handle; their hands are not big enough to hold bulky or heavy boxes like milk cartons.

- Use both hands. Ask them to use one hand to hold the handle of what they are pouring and the other hand to hold the receiving container.

- Have them hold the measuring cup as close to the bowl as possible.

- Fill a measuring cup with dried beans and let your little one pour them into a bowl. It's a fun game and a great way to practice their fine motor skills!

How to Mix, Stir, and Whisk

Give your toddler a wooden spoon, fork, or spatula and ask them to imagine that it's stuck to the bottom of the bowl. Ask them to move it around in circles slowly while keeping it close to the bottom of the bowl. This will help you avoid getting flour all over the place!

Whisking requires a slightly different movement. Ask your toddler to touch the bottom of the bowl with the whisk and then make small circles up and down—but not too high in the air, or it will spill out.

GET READY TO GET MESSY

I'm not going to lie: Baking with kids will get messy! But baking together is so fun, and the memories you create will last a lifetime. Take it from someone who loves a clean and tidy kitchen—it's totally worth it!

Here are a few extra tips to keep cleanup simple:

Dress for the mess. I recommend wearing aprons and short or rolled-up sleeves, as well as tying back long hair.

How to Knead

Kneading can be a relaxing activity. You can start kneading at the beginning, when the dough is sticky. As the gluten develops and the dough becomes elastic and less tacky, your little helper can take over. There are so many ways to knead. I usually position my palm in the center of the dough, gently press down to stretch it away from me, and then fold the dough back on itself. Turn the dough 90 degrees and repeat. I tell my kids that we are giving the dough a massage—they love that!

How to Roll

Kids tend to use more pressure on one side, causing the dough to bunch, stick, and become uneven. Remind them to roll gently and slowly. Help them rotate and flip the dough every few rolls so the surface stays even. Another trick to help prevent sticking is to place the dough between two pieces of parchment paper.

Use kid-friendly materials. To avoid breakage, try to use silicone, stainless steel, bamboo, and plastic materials.

Make cleanup fun. Invite your little helper to be part of the cleanup crew. They can place used cups, bowls, and spoons in the sink or dishwasher. When the cake is in the oven, turn the music on, pass out cleaning cloths, dustpans, and brooms. The cleanup party is on!

TIPS FOR BAKING TOGETHER

If you're worried that your little one is too young to bake, or that your kitchen will be in total shambles, give this section a read. I'll share my tips on how to approach baking so you can have the most fun and end up with yummy baked goods, not meltdowns. Feel free to adapt these tips to suit your situation.

Let your toddler choose the recipe, with guidance. Whenever I bring home a new cookbook, I love to sit down with my kids and flip through the photos and recipes. They use sticky notes to tag all the recipes they want to try. I consider the difficulty levels and what ingredients we have at home, and let them choose between my "final two." When little ones feel like they have a choice and a sense of ownership, they're much more likely to be engaged in the process.

Tell them the plan. Once you decide what to bake together, tell your toddler when you will do it. Kids like to know their daily schedule; it is reassuring and gives them structure. Knowing that the baking party will happen "after nap-time" will also give you some leverage for good behavior. Because a toddler's sense of time is limited, it's best to tell them about the baking fun on the morning of the event.

Preparation, preparation, preparation! Surprises happen! Read and reread the recipe before you start baking. Make sure you have all the necessary ingredients and tools. Review the tips in the recipe so you have time to figure out what shortcuts or changes you might want to make. Knowing what's to come will help you later, when your attention is focused on guiding your little baker.

Give yourself abundant time. Patience and time are the most important ingredients for a good bake. Any activity with toddlers needs to be done at their pace. Usually bake muffins in less than an hour? You may want to set aside double that time when you have your toddler helping you. It's better to be realistic than stressed halfway through when you're running out of time.

Set some ground rules. Before starting, remind your little helper of the basic safety rules (see page 5) to avoid any ouchies. Remind them that cleaning up is part of the baking party, too!

Set up an assembly line. If your child is very young or new to baking, or if you're pressed for time, prepare all the ingredients and pre-measure everything into little bowls, and line up all the tools on the countertop ahead of time.

Follow their lead, sort of. Even though the recipe steps say Kid Step or Adult Step, a Kid Step may require your help, or your little helper may be ready to build their skills by assisting with an Adult Step under your supervision—you know best!

Have a backup plan. Losing your child's interest doesn't mean that baking together was a failure, or that you can't try again another time. Having a Plan B can help: something to entertain your toddler while you finish up. Here are some ideas:

- If the recipe allows, pull off a small piece of dough for them to play with, such as pizza dough. Just nothing containing raw eggs!

- Give them something to snack on and play with—blueberries are awesome. They can pile them up, count them, create funny faces with them, and eat them.

- Magnets on the fridge or toys in their dedicated "kids' drawer" are fun distractions. Pull out some favorite art supplies if you have a kids' corner set up.

- Have your little one set up a pretend tea party for their dolls or stuffed animals in anticipation of the soon-to-come yummy baked treats.

Knowing that I had a Plan B in place while baking with my kids made everything way easier. As soon as they lost interest, I would give them a break. Sometimes they'd want to come back and help me finish up; other times, they'd just keep playing.

Abort mission! If your little one is just having "one of those days," simply postpone the baking party and go cuddle up on the couch with a good book or take a walk outside. A good mood is the magic ingredient in baking—and in life.

Embrace the perfectly imperfect. Cookies will be random sizes and shapes, more sprinkles might end up on the floor than on the cake, and pizza toppings might be overly concentrated in one spot. This is part of the beauty of baking with kids. Focus on the giggles, the joy, and the experience. As long as the final result is edible, who cares?

Cakes, Scones, and Muffins

2

Cakes, scones, muffins: We are definitely in the happy, fluffy, puffy, soft world here! The Sunshine Muffins (page 29) or the Lemon-Blueberry Cake (page 27) are great nutritious breakfast ideas. Bake them the day before and store on the countertop until ready to enjoy. Planning a kids' party (or pretend party) celebrating your little one's stuffed animal birthday? If so, the Strawberry Cupcakes with Whipped Cream (page 32) are a must, with their lovely fresh and light taste that the stuffed animals—and the rest of the human family—will appreciate.

Level 1

Active time: 25 minutes
Cook time: 25 minutes, plus
10 minutes to cool

Nut-Free, Vegetarian

Makes 12 muffins

We made this recipe on:

We enjoyed:

We rate this recipe:

☆ ☆ ☆ ☆ ☆

Recipe notes:

CHEESY TOMATO CORN MUFFINS

These savory corn muffins are easy to make and deliciously healthy! Cherry tomatoes are great for this recipe—they add beautiful color, and their sweetness stands up well to the nutty taste of cornmeal. The cheddar cheese offers a lovely cheesy flavor, beloved by kids everywhere! Cut up cherry tomatoes into smaller pieces to snack on as you bake together. You can use frozen corn as well; there's no need to thaw it. If you have fresh corn, sauté it for a few minutes to par-cook it first.

⅔ cup cornmeal

⅔ cup all-purpose flour

1 teaspoon baking powder

½ teaspoon baking soda

¼ teaspoon salt

½ cup extra-virgin olive oil

½ cup whole milk

2 medium eggs

1 cup grated cheddar cheese

1 cup halved cherry tomatoes

⅔ cup canned corn, rinsed and drained

1 Preheat the oven to 400°F. Line a 12-cup muffin tin with paper or silicone liners.

2 In a large bowl, gently whisk together the cornmeal, flour, baking powder, baking soda, and salt. Mix in the olive oil, milk, and eggs until well combined.

3 Add the cheese and mix until well combined. Add the tomatoes and corn and mix well.

4 Fill the muffin cups about two-thirds full. Bake for 20 to 25 minutes. Let the muffins cool for 10 minutes before enjoying warm.

Heads Up

Cornmeal has a very distinctive, grainy texture. I think it's what makes this muffin so tasty—but some toddlers might disagree! If that's the case, simply skip the cornmeal and increase the all-purpose flour to 1⅓ cups total.

Make It Fun!

Toddlers love everything mini-size! Make these mini muffins by baking in a mini muffin tin. Reduce the bake time to 10 to 15 minutes. I would suggest not using liners but to grease the muffin tin with 1 or 2 teaspoons of olive oil and to chop the tomatoes in quarters rather than in half.

MIX IT UP

Sweet Pepper Corn Muffins

Swap the cherry tomatoes for 3 sweet mini bell peppers, red and orange, seeds and pith removed and minced. Bake as directed.

Peach, Blueberry, and Orange Corn Muffins

Corn muffins can be sweet, too! Swap the olive oil for melted coconut oil, and add ½ cup of maple syrup, and increase the all-purpose flour to 1 cup. Skip the cheese, corn, and tomatoes. Instead, mix in ½ cup of peeled and chopped peaches, ½ cup of fresh blueberries, and the zest of 1 orange. Bake as directed.

LEMON-BLUEBERRY CAKE

This easy cake is perfect for beginners! The delightful combo of lemon and blueberries make this cake perfect for a special afternoon snack or even breakfast. Blueberries do double duty, as they help entertain toddlers while baking. Toddlers can count them, make shapes with them, and snack on them, too. If you can't find fresh blueberries, you can always use frozen ones. No need to thaw; just add them frozen. They will be more watery, so add 2 more tablespoons of flour and 5 more minutes to the baking time.

4 tablespoons melted coconut oil, plus 1 tablespoon for greasing

1 cup all-purpose flour

½ cup whole-wheat flour

1 teaspoon baking powder

½ teaspoon baking soda

¼ teaspoon salt

2 medium eggs

½ cup maple syrup

4 tablespoons (½ stick) unsalted butter, melted

1 tablespoon vanilla extract

Zest of 1 medium lemon

1½ cups fresh blueberries

1 Preheat the oven to 400°F and grease an 8-inch round baking pan with 1 tablespoon of coconut oil.

2 In a medium bowl, mix together the all-purpose flour, whole-wheat flour, baking powder, baking soda, and salt. Set aside.

There's more ➡

Level 1

Active time: 20 minutes
Cook time: 45 minutes, plus 10 minutes to cool

Nut-Free, Vegetarian

Serves 8

We made this recipe on:

We enjoyed:

We rate this recipe:

☆ ☆ ☆ ☆ ☆

Recipe notes:

3 In a large bowl, whisk together the eggs and maple syrup for 1 minute or until the mixture is fluffy and pale yellow. Add the butter, the remaining 4 tablespoons of coconut oil, the vanilla, and the lemon zest. Whisk to combine.

4 Slowly incorporate the dry ingredients into the wet ingredients and mix to combine. Transfer the batter into the baking pan.

5 Top the batter with the fresh blueberries. They will slowly sink by themselves.

6 Bake for 45 minutes or until a toothpick inserted in the center comes out clean. Let cool, slice, and enjoy!

MIX IT UP

Vanilla-Apricot Cake

Substitute the lemon zest with the seeds scraped from one vanilla bean. (I highly suggest using whole vanilla beans rather than vanilla extract for their flavor, but you can use 3 teaspoons of vanilla extract in a pinch.) Swap the blueberries with the same amount of in-season diced apricots—taste one to make sure they're ripe and sweet. Bake as directed.

Plum Squares

Make the batter the same way, but skip the blueberries. Transfer the batter to an 8-inch-square baking pan. Pit and halve 6 medium plums and top the batter with the plum halves, leaving a good inch in between them. Green plums (greengage variety) are our favorites, because they're sweet and not too tangy. Bake as directed, then cut into squares, each with a plum in the center.

SUNSHINE MUFFINS

These Sunshine Muffins are such a tasty and healthy way to start the day. They're moist, delicately sweet, and definitely orange, thanks to the carrots. The spice blend is like a warm hug of comforting flavors in your mouth. For this recipe I don't use liners—the batter sticks to the paper and it's tricky to separate. If you want liners, you can place the cooled muffins into liners or use silicone liners greased with coconut oil.

2 tablespoons melted coconut oil, plus 1 tablespoon coconut oil for greasing

2 cups whole-wheat flour

1½ teaspoons baking powder

1 teaspoon ground cinnamon

½ teaspoon baking soda

¼ teaspoon ground nutmeg

¼ teaspoon ground cardamom

¼ teaspoon salt

½ cup maple syrup

2 medium eggs

1 tablespoon vanilla extract

½ cup plain Greek yogurt

¼ cup whole milk

2 cups finely grated carrots

1 Preheat the oven to 425°F and grease a 12-cup muffin tin with 1 tablespoon of coconut oil.

2 In a medium bowl, mix together the flour, baking powder, cinnamon, baking soda, nutmeg, cardamom, and salt until well combined. Set aside.

There's more

Level 1

Active time: 20 minutes
Cook time: 25 minutes, plus
10 minutes to cool

Nut-Free, Vegetarian

Makes 12 muffins

We made this recipe on:

We enjoyed:

We rate this recipe:

☆ ☆ ☆ ☆ ☆

Recipe notes:

3 In a large bowl, whisk together the maple syrup, eggs, the remaining 2 tablespoons of coconut oil, and the vanilla. Stir in the yogurt and milk.

4 Slowly add the flour mixture into the wet ingredients, a few spoonfuls at a time. Mix well. Fold in the grated carrots until just combined.

5 Fill the muffin cups three-quarters of the way full with batter. Bake for 5 minutes. Reduce the temperature to 350°F and bake for another 15 to 18 minutes, or until the tops feel firm and a toothpick inserted in the center comes out clean. Let cool for 10 minutes. Enjoy!

Make It Fun!

While the muffins are baking, have your little ones look for as many orange objects they can find. Older kids can find objects starting with "O" for orange and "C" for carrot. Then enjoy the muffins together while reading a good book like *T-Veg: The Tale of a Carrot-Crunching Dinosaur*, a beautiful tale about dinosaurs, carrot cakes, and embracing differences.

MIX IT UP

Cranberry-Carrot Bran Muffins

For an extra boost of iron and fiber, reduce the whole-wheat flour to 1 cup and add 1 cup of wheat bran. Pulse the bran in a food processor until it's the consistency of bread crumbs. Substitute the spices with ½ cup of dried cranberries. Bake as directed.

Muffin Ice-Cream Cones

You'll need small, flat-bottomed ice-cream cones. Fill them three-quarters full with the batter. To stabilize them, use a small baking pan and tightly line them up next to each other. You can also put the cones in the cups of a muffin tin and wrap aluminum foil around the base of each cone to keep them steady. Bake at 350°F for 20 to 23 minutes. Decorate with a drizzle of melted chocolate and dye-free sprinkles.

Level 2

Active time: 45 minutes
Cook time: 40 minutes
(20 minutes per batch),
plus 10 minutes to cool

Nut-Free, Vegetarian

Makes 18 cupcakes

We made this recipe on:

We enjoyed:

We rate this recipe:

☆ ☆ ☆ ☆ ☆

Recipe notes:

STRAWBERRY CUPCAKES WITH WHIPPED CREAM

There's always a good reason to make these celebratory cupcakes—a birthday, Grandma coming to visit, or just because it's a sunny day! These cupcakes contain fresh strawberries for a naturally fruity flavor and a lovely pink color. Although they take a bit of time to prepare, the kid steps are fairly simple. The cupcakes are topped with a light, homemade whipped cream.

For the cupcakes

6 large fresh whole strawberries, plus 9 halved strawberries for garnish

1½ cups all-purpose flour

1½ teaspoons baking powder

½ teaspoon baking soda

½ teaspoon salt

½ cup (1 stick) unsalted butter, at room temperature

¾ cup maple syrup

2 teaspoons vanilla extract

2 medium eggs

½ cup plain Greek yogurt

¼ cup whole milk

For the whipped cream

2 cups cold (heavy) whipping cream

¼ cup maple syrup

1 tablespoon vanilla extract

There's more

Heads Up

To make it more manageable, spread this cupcake-making activity across two days. Prepare and bake the cupcake batter the first day. The next day, prepare the whipped cream and decorate the cupcakes.

To make the cupcakes

1 Preheat the oven to 350°F. Line a 12-cup muffin tin and a 6-cup muffin tin.

2 In a food processor or blender, purée 6 strawberries until smooth. Set aside.

3 In a medium bowl, whisk together the flour, baking powder, baking soda, and salt until well combined. Set aside.

4 In a large bowl, using an electric hand mixer, cream together the butter and maple syrup for about 3 minutes, or until airy and fluffy. If your little helper wants to assist, remind them to keep the beaters close to the bottom of the bowl.

5 Add the vanilla and eggs and whisk for 1 minute. Scrape the sides of the bowl if needed.

6 Slowly add the dry ingredients into the egg mixture, alternating with the yogurt and milk. Whisk until well combined. Add the strawberry purée and mix well.

7 Fill the liners about two-thirds full. Bake for 20 minutes. Let the cupcakes cool for 10 minutes.

To make the whipped cream

8 In a chilled bowl, using an electric hand mixer, beat together the heavy cream, maple syrup, and vanilla for 2 minutes. Start on low and increase to high as stiff peaks form.

9 Transfer the whipped cream to a piping bag fitted with your desired tip. Frost the cupcakes and top each with a strawberry half.

MIX IT UP

Chocolate Cupcakes with Whipped Cream

Add 2 tablespoons of unsweetened cocoa powder to the flour mixture, and substitute the strawberry purée in the batter with ¾ cup of chocolate chips. Top the cupcakes with chocolate chips or chopped nuts instead of strawberries. Bake as directed.

Strawberry Cake Pops

Mash leftover cupcakes and whipped cream in a bowl to create a sticky mix. Coat your hands with some coconut oil, and roll 1 tablespoon of the mix into a ball. Roll the cake balls in coconut flakes, chopped nuts, or dye-free sprinkles, or drizzle with melted chocolate. Insert a lollipop stick in the center of each ball. Place on a lined baking tray. Refrigerate for at least 30 minutes.

PARMESAN SCONES WITH FRESH HERBS

A savory scone is like a crumbly, tender biscuit or quick bread—and this flavor-loaded combination of Parmesan, olives, and fresh herbs is like Italy in a bite. I enjoy the triangular shape of traditional scones, but for little hands, a simple round scone is easier to shape and hold.

2½ cups all-purpose flour

¾ cup grated Parmesan cheese, divided

2½ teaspoons baking powder

½ teaspoon salt

½ cup (1 stick) unsalted butter, frozen and cut into tiny cubes

½ cup whole milk

½ cup pitted green or black olives, minced

2 tablespoons minced marjoram, thyme, or oregano (or any combination of the three)

1 Preheat the oven to 400°F. Line a baking sheet with parchment paper.

2 In a large bowl, mix together the flour, ½ cup of Parmesan cheese, the baking powder, and salt with a fork until well combined.

3 Add the cold butter and work it into the flour mixture with your hands until it's a wet sand texture, about 2 minutes.

Level 3

Active time: 20 minutes
Cook time: 25 minutes,
plus 10 minutes to cool

Egg-Free, Nut-Free, Vegetarian

Makes 12 scones

We made this recipe on:

We enjoyed:

We rate this recipe:

☆ ☆ ☆ ☆ ☆

Recipe notes:

There's more ➡

4 Slowly add the milk and mix with a fork until the milk is absorbed into the flour. Use your hands to form the ingredients into a compact dough.

5 Add the olives and fresh herbs. Knead the dough for 1 minute to evenly distribute the ingredients.

6 Take 1 heaping spoonful of the dough and roll it into a ball. Place the ball on the prepared baking sheet. Gently press down on the ball with your palm to flatten to about 1-inch thickness. Repeat with the remaining dough to make 12 scones.

7 Sprinkle 1 teaspoon of the remaining Parmesan cheese on top of each scone.

8 Bake for 25 minutes. Let cool for 10 minutes, then enjoy!

Baker's Tip

Cold butter is essential for tender, flaky scones. Finely cube the frozen butter while your little helper removes the leaves from the herbs. Refrigerate the cubes while you finish the ingredient prep. Remove the butter from the fridge right before you add it to the flour mixture.

MIX IT UP

Dried Cranberries and Orange Scones

For a sweet and fruity scone, swap out the Parmesan cheese for maple syrup, the olives for dried cranberries, and the fresh herbs for orange zest, all in the same quantities. Bake as directed.

Basil Pesto and Sun-Dried Tomato Scones

This combo delivers an intense flavor, but you might be surprised by how much your little one loves it! Add 3 tablespoons of basil pesto right after the milk. Substitute the same amount of chopped sun-dried tomatoes for the olives and use only oregano for the herbs. Bake as directed.

Breads, Biscuits, and Pizza

3

I don't know a single kid who doesn't like bread in any of its forms: loaf, panini, buns, pizza, breadstick, pretzel—yum! It's such a simple, basic food that's a pleasure to eat and bake. I suggest that your little bakers start with the Easy-Peasy Cheese Pizza (page 45) and then move up to the Twisty Pretzel Circles (page 48) or, for a sweet note, the Cherry Focaccia (page 54). If you don't have time to let the yeast do its magic, skip it and enjoy the Super Speedy Flatbread (page 51).

Active time: 20 minutes
Cook time: 50 minutes,
plus 10 minutes to cool

Nut-Free, Vegetarian

Makes 1 (9-by-5-inch) loaf

We made this recipe on:

We enjoyed:

We rate this recipe:

☆ ☆ ☆ ☆ ☆

Recipe notes:

PUMPKIN AND CHOCOLATE CHIP QUICK BREAD

This moist, flavorful, and healthy pumpkin bread is delicately spiced with cinnamon, nutmeg, ginger, and cloves—it just makes me think of fall! The pumpkin purée gives this bread a creamy sweetness that kids love. Make sure you don't accidentally buy pumpkin pie filling, which is already sweetened. I added some chocolate chips, because as my little one says, "chocolate is the best."

¼ cup coconut oil or unsalted butter, melted, plus more for greasing

2 cups whole-wheat flour

1 teaspoon baking powder

1 teaspoon baking soda

1 teaspoon salt

1 teaspoon ground cinnamon

½ teaspoon ground nutmeg

¼ teaspoon ground cloves

⅛ teaspoon ground ginger

1 tablespoon lemon zest

½ cup granulated cane or coconut sugar

½ cup maple syrup

2 medium eggs

1 cup canned pumpkin purée

½ cup whole milk

1 teaspoon vanilla extract

½ cup mini semisweet chocolate chips, plus more for topping

1. Preheat the oven to 350°F. Grease a 9-by-5-inch loaf pan with coconut oil.

2. In a medium bowl, mix together the flour, baking powder, baking soda, salt, cinnamon, nutmeg, cloves, ginger, and lemon zest. Set aside.

3. In a large bowl, whisk together the coconut sugar, maple syrup, remaining ¼ cup of coconut oil, and the eggs for 1 minute, until the mixture is pale and well blended. Add the pumpkin purée, milk, and vanilla and mix until well combined.

4. Slowly combine the dry ingredients into the wet mixture, a few spoonfuls at a time. Whisk until just combined. Pour the batter into the loaf pan.

5. Decorate the top with some chocolate chips. (Don't forget to try one or two just to make sure the chocolate is good enough!)

6. Bake the pumpkin bread for 45 to 50 minutes, or until a toothpick inserted into the center comes out clean. Let cool for 10 minutes. Slice and enjoy!

Heads Up

Yes, your little one can help combine dry ingredients with the wet ones without flour going everywhere! Ask them to slowly whisk the wet ingredients in the large bowl while you carefully add a few spoonfuls of the dry mixture. Remind them to keep the whisk close to the bottom of the bowl.

MIX IT UP

Nutty Banana Bread

All the little monkeys in my life love banana bread! Swap the cup of pumpkin purée for 3 mashed medium, ripe bananas. Substitute the chocolate chips with chopped walnuts, or don't substitute and simply add them for a richer and chunkier result. Bake as directed.

Cheesy Zucchini Bread

This savory bread is a great way to get kids to try zucchini! Substitute the pumpkin purée with a packed cup of finely grated zucchini (squeeze out all the extra water). Skip the coconut sugar, maple syrup, cinnamon, nutmeg, ginger, clove, lemon zest, and chocolate chips. Instead, add ½ cup of grated aged Asiago, Manchego, or sharp cheddar cheese. Bake as directed.

Level 1

Active time: 25 minutes
Cook time: 10 minutes,
plus 10 minutes to cool

Egg-Free, Nut-Free, Vegetarian

Makes 8

We made this recipe on:

We enjoyed:

We rate this recipe:

☆ ☆ ☆ ☆ ☆

Recipe notes:

BISCUITS WITH RASPBERRY CHIA JAM

These deliciously airy and fluffy biscuits are the perfect vehicle for this tasty raspberry chia seed jam. If you make the jam ahead of time, you can enjoy these warm biscuits for an afternoon snack with your little ones (and maybe a few stuffed animal friends) in no time.

For the jam

2 cups fresh raspberries

3 tablespoons maple syrup

2 tablespoons chia seeds

For the biscuits

2 cups all-purpose flour

2 teaspoons baking powder

½ teaspoon salt

4 tablespoons (½ stick) unsalted butter, frozen and cut into cubes

¾ cup plain Greek yogurt

To make the jam

1. In a saucepan, cook the raspberries over medium heat for 2 minutes, mashing them with a spoon. Turn off the heat and stir in the maple syrup and chia seeds. Let it cool while you make the biscuits.

There's more

Heads Up

Knives are a top concern when cooking with kids. They are also one of the most useful tools in the kitchen. You can start practicing with these delicious biscuits and a safe butter knife (see page 7 for tips). After you help them cut their biscuit in half, they can practice spreading the jam on top.

To make the biscuits

2 Preheat the oven to 450°F. Line a baking sheet with parchment paper.

3 In a food processor, combine the flour, baking powder, salt, and butter. Pulse for 30 seconds, or until the mixture has a sandy texture.

4 Transfer the mix to a clean, flat surface, and make a well in the center. Add the yogurt into the well, and slowly incorporate the flour and butter mixture with the yogurt. Use your hands to bring it together into a ball, making sure not to overwork it.

5 With a rolling pin, roll out the dough into a 1½-inch-thick layer. Using a 3-inch round cookie cutter or inverted glass, cut out 8 biscuits, reforming and rerolling the dough to use every scrap.

6 Place the biscuits on the prepared baking sheet. Bake for 10 minutes, or until lightly browned. Let cool for 10 minutes.

7 Using a butter knife, cut open the biscuit and spread the raspberry jam on top (see Heads Up tip). Enjoy!

MIX IT UP

Sun-Dried Tomato and Parmesan Biscuits

For a savory twist, add ½ cup of grated Parmesan cheese, ½ cup of minced sun-dried tomatoes, and 5 finely chopped basil leaves with the yogurt. Bake as directed.

Almond Flour Biscuits

Substitute the all-purpose flour with almond flour and add 2 medium eggs to the mix with the yogurt. These biscuits are gluten-free, with a hint of deliciously nutty flavor. Bake as directed.

EASY-PEASY CHEESE PIZZA

I've never known a kid to turn down pizza night! This simple pizza dough doesn't need a stand mixer, requires minimal prep, and takes only an hour to rest. It's the perfect Saturday afternoon activity. I've kept the toppings basic, too—just sauce, cheese, and a little olive oil. But go ahead and portion out the dough into four pieces to make four small pizzas, set out a toppings bar, and let everyone create their own!

For the dough

4 cups all-purpose flour

1 teaspoon instant yeast

1 tablespoon sea salt

1 teaspoon sugar

1¼ cups lukewarm water

¼ cup extra-virgin olive oil

Cornmeal flour, for dusting

For the pizza

¼ cup extra-virgin olive oil, plus 2 tablespoons for greasing

¾ cup tomato sauce or marinara

1 cup cubed low-moisture mozzarella

To make the dough

1 In a large bowl, stir together the flour, yeast, salt, and sugar. Slowly pour the lukewarm water and ¼ cup of olive oil in the center and mix with a fork until you have a sticky dough.

Level 1

Active time: 30 minutes
Rest time: 1 hour
Cook time: 20 minutes

Egg-Free, Nut-Free, Vegetarian

Serves 4

We made this recipe on:

We enjoyed:

We rate this recipe:

☆ ☆ ☆ ☆ ☆

Recipe notes:

There's more ➡

2 Transfer the dough to a clean, flat surface dusted with cornmeal flour. With clean hands, gather the dough into a ball, pressing and reshaping until it loses some of its stickiness. Knead for about 5 minutes, or until the dough is elastic and shiny. Alternate kneading with your little helper, or cut off a small piece for them to play with while you knead.

3 Form the dough into a ball and place on a baking sheet dusted with some cornmeal flour. Cover with a damp kitchen cloth and place in the cold oven for 1 hour, or until the dough has doubled in size.

To make the pizza

4 Remove the dough from the oven and dust a flat surface with cornmeal flour. Preheat the oven to 450°F. Grease a baking sheet or pizza pan with 2 tablespoons of olive oil.

5 Using a rolling pin on a floured work surface, roll out the dough into a 12-inch disk around ¼-inch thick. Place on the prepared baking sheet.

6 Spread the tomato sauce on top of the pizza with the bottom of a tablespoon. Distribute the mozzarella cheese evenly on top.

7 Drizzle the remaining ¼ cup of olive oil over the pizza. Bake for 18 to 20 minutes, or until the cheese is melted and the pizza is lightly browned. Slice and enjoy!

MIX IT UP

Spinach-Pesto Pinwheels

Roll out the pizza dough into an ⅛-inch-thick rectangle. Spread 3 tablespoons of basil pesto over the dough, and cover with a couple handfuls of baby spinach leaves. Roll the dough into a cylinder, and cut into ½-inch slices. Place on a lined baking sheet and bake at 400°F for 18 to 20 minutes, or until golden brown.

Cheesy Breadsticks

Divide the pizza dough into 2-inch cubes. Roll each with your hands to form a breadstick, about 8 inches long. Place the breadsticks on a lined baking sheet. Stir together 5 tablespoons of olive oil, 1 teaspoon of oregano, and ½ teaspoon of salt. Brush the breadsticks with the oil mixture and sprinkle with grated Parmesan cheese. Bake at 400°F for 12 to 15 minutes, or until golden brown.

Make It Fun!

Line up 4 or 5 cups with a small amount of each topping and have everyone create their own pizza. You can also add some veggies, even in small quantities. Sometimes combining a favorite food like pizza with not-so-favorite ones helps with picky eating.

Level 2

Active time: 30 minutes
Rest time: 30 minutes
Cook time: 15 minutes,
plus 5 minutes to cool

Egg-Free, Nut-Free, Vegetarian

Makes 5 pretzel circles

We made this recipe on:

We enjoyed:

We rate this recipe:

☆☆☆☆☆

Recipe notes:

TWISTY PRETZEL CIRCLES

My kids love these buttery soft pretzels! They love pulling the pretzels apart, savoring both the crackly crust and the softer insides. You can really have fun shaping the pretzels! Use instant yeast, also known as rapid-rise yeast, to cut down on rising time so you can enjoy these delicious homemade pretzels in less time.

4 cups all-purpose flour, plus more for dusting

2 tablespoons sugar

2¼ teaspoons instant yeast

1½ teaspoons sea salt

½ cup water

1 cup whole milk

2 tablespoons extra-virgin olive oil

2 tablespoons baking soda

2 cups warm water

Coarse sea salt, for topping (optional)

1 Line 2 baking sheets with parchment paper.

2 In a large bowl, mix together the flour, sugar, yeast, and salt. Set aside.

3 In a saucepan over medium heat, warm the water, milk, and olive oil until just simmering. Turn off the heat and stir the liquid into the flour mix. Invite your little helper to watch carefully but not to get too close.

4 With a fork, mix the ingredients into a soft dough.

There's more ➡

Make It Fun!

Have fun rolling, twisting, and forming the pretzels into different shapes with your little ones! Alternatively, cut them into 1-inch bites. With older kids, you can try braiding the pretzels, or forming the classic pretzel shape. Shape your pretzel dough into letters or numbers for an edible lesson.

5 Transfer the dough to a clean, flat surface dusted with some flour. Knead the dough for 5 minutes, taking turns with your little helper. Form the dough into a ball, cover with a damp kitchen towel, and let rest for 10 minutes.

6 Cut the dough into 10 equal pieces. Roll each piece into an 8- to 10-inch stick. Curve the stick into a circle and press the ends together lightly with your thumbs to seal. Place the circles on one prepared baking sheet.

7 In a large shallow bowl, mix together the baking soda with the warm water. Dip each pretzel into the soda water and return to the lined baking sheet. Sprinkle coarse salt on top (if using). Let rest for 20 minutes.

8 Preheat the oven to 450°F.

9 Transfer the pretzels to the second lined baking sheet. Bake for 8 to 10 minutes, or until golden brown. Let cool for 5 minutes and enjoy warm!

MIX IT UP

Cheesy Seed Pretzels

Just before baking, sprinkle some grated Parmesan cheese and your choice of poppy, sunflower, or sesame seeds (or a mix!) on top. Bake as directed.

Cinnamon Sugar Pretzels

On a plate, mix together 3 tablespoons of sugar and 2 teaspoons of ground cinnamon. After dipping the pretzel in the soda water, dip them quickly in the cinnamon sugar before placing them back on the baking sheet. Bake as directed.

SUPER SPEEDY FLATBREAD

Flatbreads are one of the easiest recipes in the bread category and also one of the most versatile: It can be a snack, a sandwich wrap, creative pizza base, or a breakfast (see variation on page 53). There's no yeast or long rising time involved. The most kid-friendly filling for this flatbread is ham and cream cheese, because it's easy to handle and the filling doesn't fall out. Add a few strips of grilled zucchini to sneak in some veggies.

1 cup lukewarm water

⅓ cup extra-virgin olive oil

1 teaspoon salt

4 cups all-purpose flour, plus more for dusting

1 teaspoon baking soda

1 In a large bowl, combine the water and the olive oil. Add the salt and mix with a fork. Stir in the flour, a few tablespoons at a time. Add the baking soda. Keep stirring with the fork for 2 to 3 minutes, until a sticky dough is formed.

2 Transfer the dough onto a flat surface dusted with flour. Knead it for 3 minutes or until elastic and compact. Offer your toddler a tiny piece of dough to practice kneading. Show them how to stretch the dough with one hand and fold it back on itself.

3 Roll the dough into a ball, place it in the bowl, cover with plastic wrap, and let it rest for 15 minutes.

Level 2

Active time: 40 minutes
Rest time: 15 minutes
Cook time: 30 minutes,
plus 5 minutes to cool

Dairy-Free, Egg-Free, Nut-Free, Vegan

Makes 5 flatbreads

We made this recipe on:

We enjoyed:

We rate this recipe:

☆ ☆ ☆ ☆ ☆

Recipe notes:

There's more ➡

Baker's Tip

Because the flatbread doesn't need to rise much, it can be prepared using different flours for a gluten-free alternative. Buckwheat, rice, chickpea, coconut, and even quinoa flour are all good options. You can use a 1:1 substitution ratio.

4 Remove the dough from the bowl and roll it into a cylinder. Divide the cylinder into 5 equal parts and roll each one into a ball. Using a rolling pin, flatten each ball and roll it out into a 10-inch disk, ⅛-inch thick.

5 Heat a large nonstick skillet over medium heat. When the pan is hot, add the first flatbread. With a fork, gently poke the flatbread surface all over. Cook for 2 to 3 minutes per side. Stack the flatbreads, wrapped with a kitchen cloth, to keep them warm and soft. Enjoy!

MIX IT UP

Spinach Green, Turmeric Gold, or Tomato Red Flatbread

More color brings more fun and greater chances that kids will eat it. Make a vibrant green flatbread by blending the water with 1 cup of spinach leaves. Proceed as directed. To create a golden flatbread, mix the water with 2 teaspoons of turmeric. For a reddish flatbread, add 1 tablespoon of thick tomato paste to the water. For fun edible art, cut the colored flatbread with cookie cutters shaped like leaves and place them in a small basket, like fall leaves from the backyard! Bake as directed.

Apple Breakfast Flatbread

Save some flatbread for the next day's breakfast. Reheat the flatbread in a skillet for 30 seconds over medium heat. Spread 1 tablespoon of applesauce on each flatbread. Top with sliced banana, a pinch of cinnamon, and 1 teaspoon of hemp seeds for extra nutrition. For a party breakfast, you can drizzle on some melted chocolate, too. For little ones, fold the flatbread in half, then cut small triangles, roll it, and slice into pinwheels, or leave it open like a pizza and slice into small wedges.

CHERRY FOCACCIA

Active time: 30 minutes
Rest time: 1 hour 20 minutes
Cook time: 30 minutes

Dairy-Free, Egg-Free, Nut-Free, Vegan

Serves 8

This cherry focaccia is a delightful, sweet twist on traditional focaccia. I love using dark, super sweet cherries for this recipe—and little ones love it, too. My kids' favorite part is poking the focaccia dough to make the dimples!

1 teaspoon active dry yeast

½ cup sugar, plus 3 tablespoons, plus 1 teaspoon

1½ cups warm water

4 cups bread flour, plus more for dusting

1½ teaspoons salt

2 tablespoons extra-virgin olive oil, divided

2 cups fresh or frozen cherries, pitted

Zest of ½ medium lemon

1 In a small bowl, stir together the active yeast and 1 teaspoon of sugar with the warm water until the yeast has completely dissolved. Set aside for 5 minutes. It will foam.

2 In a large bowl, use a fork to mix together the flour, the yeast mixture, ½ cup of sugar, the salt, and 1 tablespoon of olive oil until you have a sticky dough.

3 Transfer the dough to a clean, flat surface dusted with flour. Knead for 8 to 10 minutes, or until elastic and no longer sticky. Alternate kneading with your little helper, or pinch off a little bit of dough for them to play with.

There's more

Heads Up

You can make pitting cherries fun with your kiddo. All you need are metal straws and clothes you don't mind getting dirty—cherry stains aren't so easy to remove. Hold the cherry with one hand. With the other hand, press the straw into the center of the cherry, where the stem used to be. Press down and rotate the straw like a drill. The straw will poke the pit through the other side.

4 Place the dough in another large bowl dusted with flour. Cover with plastic wrap or a silicone cover, place in the cold oven, and let it rest for 1 hour, or until the dough doubles in volume.

5 Meanwhile, in a saucepan over low heat, combine the cherries, the remaining 3 tablespoons of sugar, and the lemon zest. Cook, stirring frequently, for 3 minutes, or until thickened and reduced. Let cool for 5 minutes.

6 Grease a 9-by-13-inch baking pan with the remaining 1 tablespoon of olive oil. Transfer the focaccia dough to the pan. Preheat the oven to 400°F.

7 Using clean hands, spread the dough to fill the pan. Poke the dough with fingers to make dimples all over the surface. Spread the cherry mixture across the top of the dough, filling the dimples with cherries. Let rest on the countertop for 20 minutes.

8 Bake for 30 minutes, or until the edges and the top are golden brown.
Enjoy warm or at room temperature.

Make It Fun!

Rather than cutting your focaccia into squares after baking, use cookie cutters to stamp out cute shapes. As a bonus, you can snack on the scraps!

MIX IT UP

Zucchini and Tomato Focaccia

For a savory focaccia, omit the sugar and substitute the cherry topping with fresh zucchini and cherry tomatoes. Thinly slice 1 large zucchini. Toss the zucchini and a handful of cherry tomatoes with 1 tablespoon of olive oil and ½ teaspoon of salt. Spread the mixture on top of the focaccia, let rest, and then bake as directed.

Pineapple and Blueberries Focaccia

Instead of the cherry topping, mix 1 cup of chopped fresh pineapple and 1 cup of fresh blueberries with ½ cup of maple syrup and 1 teaspoon of finely chopped mint. Spread on top of the focaccia, let rest, and then bake as directed.

Cookies, Crackers, and Bars

4

Whether you want to offer a quick snack at home or an on-the-go treat, cookies, crackers, and bars are always a hit. The Oat-So-Easy Chocolate Chip Cookies (page 60) and the Chocolate-Almond Thumbprint Cookies (page 65) are a hit with chocolate-loving kids. The Strawberry Ravioli Cookies (page 68) are perfect for a cozy afternoon baking party—your toddler will love sealing the "ravioli" with a fork. And if your sweet tooth has been satisfied, try the savory Cheddar-Almond Crackers (page 71). They go perfectly with some cut-up grapes.

Level 1

Active time: 25 minutes
Cook time: 25 minutes
(12 minutes per batch),
plus 5 minutes to cool

Dairy-Free, Nut-Free, Vegetarian

Makes 25 to 30 cookies

We made this recipe on:

We enjoyed:

We rate this recipe:

☆☆☆☆☆

Recipe notes:

OAT-SO-EASY CHOCOLATE CHIP COOKIES

Chocolate chip cookies? That's a recipe that gets everyone on board. It's also one of the easiest to prepare and a perfect recipe to start baking with your toddler. I use a 1:1 ratio of whole-wheat flour and rolled oats to give the cookies a lighter texture, and blend the oats for a smoother, toddler-friendly texture. If your toddler enjoys chunky cookies, skip the blender and just add the oats as is.

1 cup rolled oats

1 cup whole-wheat flour

½ teaspoon baking soda

¼ teaspoon salt

1 medium egg

½ cup sugar

¼ cup coconut oil, melted

1 tablespoon vanilla extract

¾ cup dark chocolate chips

1 Preheat the oven to 350°F. Line 2 baking sheets with parchment paper.

2 In a food processor, blend the oats for about 1 minute, until you achieve a flour-like texture.

3 In a medium bowl, mix together the blended oats, whole-wheat flour, baking soda, and salt with a fork until well combined.

4 In a large bowl, whisk together the egg and sugar for 1 minute, or until well combined. Add the coconut oil and vanilla and whisk to combine.

5. Slowly add the dry ingredients to the wet ingredients. Scrape down the sides of the bowl as needed. Add the chocolate chips and stir until just combined.

6. Scoop up about 1 tablespoon of dough. Use clean hands to roll it into a ball and place on a lined baking sheet. Gently press down to flatten a bit. Leave 2 inches in between each cookie.

7. Bake for 12 minutes, or until golden brown on top. Allow to cool and firm up for 5 minutes. Repeat with the remaining batter and second baking sheet. Enjoy!

Baker's Tip

You can easily freeze these cookies before baking them. Place the flattened balls of dough on a small tray and freeze, then transfer to a resealable freezer bag. Freeze for up to 3 months. When ready to bake, place the frozen cookies on a lined baking sheet and bake at 350°F for 15 minutes. You can also freeze the baked cookies. Just thaw in the refrigerator overnight or microwave for 40 seconds.

MIX IT UP

Banana-Almond Chocolate Chip Cookies

For a richer, egg-free alternative, swap the egg for one mashed medium, ripe banana, and substitute the oats for ½ cup of almond meal. Bake as directed.

Coconut-Cinnamon Raisin Cookies

Swap the chocolate chips for raisins, and mix in ½ cup of coconut flakes and ½ teaspoon of cinnamon. To avoid chewy raisins, soak them in warm water for 30 minutes before adding. Bake as directed.

RASPBERRY-ORANGE OAT BARS

These fruity, crumbly squares are the perfect addition to a backyard tea party with friends (or some lucky stuffed animals)! For an extra fun touch, wrap the bars in strips of parchment paper and seal them with a bit of colorful tape.

½ cup coconut oil, melted

¼ cup sugar

¼ cup maple syrup

2 teaspoons vanilla extract

1 cup whole-wheat flour

½ teaspoon baking soda

¼ teaspoon ground nutmeg

¼ teaspoon salt

1 cup rolled oats

1 cup raspberry jam

Zest of 1 medium orange, and 2 tablespoons of the juice

1 Preheat the oven to 350°F and line a 13-by-9-inch baking dish with parchment paper.

2 In a large bowl, stir together the coconut oil, sugar, maple syrup, and vanilla until well combined.

3 Add the flour, baking soda, nutmeg, and salt and mix well. Add the oats and combine well.

There's more

Baker's Tip

The pan needs to be completely cool before you slice the bars, or they will be a crumbly mess! You can also place the cooled pan in the refrigerator for 30 minutes before slicing.

4 Reserve 1 cup of the crumble mixture, and transfer the rest to the prepared baking pan. Place a piece of parchment paper on top of the crumble.

5 Using your hands, push down on the parchment paper to press the crumble evenly into the bottom of the pan. When the mixture is very compact, remove the parchment paper.

6 In a medium bowl, mix together the raspberry jam with the orange zest and juice. Using a small spoon, spread it on top of the crumble crust. Sprinkle the reserved crumble mixture on top.

7 Bake for 30 minutes, or until the crumble is golden brown. Let it cool completely, about an hour, before slicing it into bars.

MIX IT UP

Chocolate Oat Bars

Swap the raspberry-orange mixture for ¾ cup of chocolate hazelnut spread and ¼ cup of milk. You can warm the spread in the microwave for 10 seconds so it's easier to mix. Drizzle the chocolate mixture over the crust and proceed as directed.

Tropical Oat Bars

Substitute the raspberry-orange jam with a mango-pineapple spread. Blend ½ cup of mango and ½ cup of pineapple for 1 minute or until smooth. Stir in 1½ tablespoons of chia seeds and let it thicken for 5 minutes. Frozen or canned fruit will work just as well as fresh. You can also substitute the nutmeg with cardamom; it works well with the tropical flavors! Bake as directed.

CHOCOLATE-ALMOND THUMBPRINT COOKIES

Thumbprint cookies are a fun hands-on recipe to prepare with your toddlers. These nutty shortbread cookies will melt in your mouth, and you can personalize the filling following your little one's taste.

1 medium, ripe banana

1½ cups almond meal or almond flour

1½ cups all-purpose unbleached flour

½ cup sugar

1 teaspoon baking soda

¼ teaspoon salt

2 tablespoons melted coconut oil or unsalted butter, plus more for greasing

2 tablespoons unsweetened applesauce

1 tablespoon vanilla extract

5 tablespoons chocolate hazelnut spread

1. Preheat the oven to 400°F and line 2 baking sheets with parchment paper.

2. Peel the banana and break it into chunks. Place the pieces in a shallow bowl and mash them into a paste with a fork.

3. In a large bowl, use a fork to mix together the almond meal, flour, sugar, baking soda, and salt until well combined.

4. Slowly pour in the coconut oil, applesauce, mashed banana, and vanilla. Mix with a wooden spoon for 1 or 2 minutes, until the dough is compact and sticky.

There's more

Level 2

Prep time: 30 minutes
Cook time: 40 minutes
(20 minutes per batch),
plus 5 minutes to cool

Egg-Free, Vegetarian

Makes 25 to 30 cookies

We made this recipe on:

We enjoyed:

We rate this recipe:

☆ ☆ ☆ ☆ ☆

Recipe notes:

5. Grease your clean hands with coconut oil. Scoop 1 tablespoon of dough with a spoon and roll it into a small ball. Place the ball on the parchment paper. Repeat with the remaining dough, placing 2 inches apart.

6. Gently press your thumb in the center of each ball. Fill each indent with ½ teaspoon of chocolate hazelnut spread.

7. Bake for 20 minutes, or until golden brown. Let cool for 5 minutes before enjoying.

Heads Up

Your little helper's thumb might be too small to leave a print big enough for the filling. They can also use the back of a measuring teaspoon.

MIX IT UP

Sprinkle Cookies

Add some festive color with seasonally appropriate sprinkles! Skip the indent filled with chocolate hazelnut spread. Set out small bowls with different colored sprinkles, and let your toddler choose how to coat each dough ball. Bake as directed.

Fruity Thumbprint Cookies

Fill the center with ½ teaspoon of fruit jam and top with a small piece of fresh fruit. I love raspberry jam and banana, blueberry jam with strawberries, or applesauce and kiwi, or let your kiddo come up with their favorite combinations! Bake as directed.

Prep time: 30 minutes
Rest time: 30 minutes
Cook time: 40 minutes
(20 minutes per batch),
plus 10 minutes to cool

Dairy-Free, Nut-Free, Vegetarian

Makes 30 ravioli

We made this recipe on:

We enjoyed:

We rate this recipe:

☆ ☆ ☆ ☆ ☆

Recipe notes:

STRAWBERRY RAVIOLI COOKIES

This sweet interpretation of ravioli involves a buttery shortbread dough filled with a jammy strawberry mixture—just like little treasure chests of flavor! We use strawberries, but peaches are great in the summer, or pears or figs in the fall. You can also swap out the jam for chocolate spread. Let your little ones decide!

½ cup strawberries, diced

½ cup strawberry jam

2¼ cups all-purpose flour

1 medium egg

4 tablespoons (½ stick) unsalted butter, softened

4 tablespoons sugar

5 tablespoons milk of your choice

Zest of 1 lemon

½ teaspoon baking powder

1 Preheat the oven to 350°F and line 2 baking sheets with parchment paper.

2 In a small bowl, mash the strawberries with a fork until chunky. Stir in the strawberry jam and set aside.

3 In a large bowl, use a fork to mix together the flour, egg, butter, sugar, milk, lemon zest, and baking powder until it forms a dough. Transfer to a clean, flat surface and use clean hands to knead it for 1 minute.

4 Wrap the dough in plastic wrap and let it rest on the countertop for 30 minutes.

There's more

Heads Up

Cookie dough is perfect for rolling pin practice! Show your little one how to roll the pin slowly and lightly over the dough. They can practice with the scraps while you finish cutting out the cookies. You might not end up with as many cookies, but it's worth it!

5 Using a rolling pin, roll out the dough to about ⅛-inch thick. Using a 4-inch round cookie cutter or a glass, cut out circles of dough. Gather up the dough scraps and roll out again to cut out more disks. Repeat with remaining dough. This should yield about 30 circles.

6 Place 1 teaspoon of strawberry mix in the center of each disk and gently fold it on itself, creating a half-moon. Press the edges with fingers or a fork to seal.

7 Place 15 ravioli on each baking sheet, leaving a bit of space between the ravioli. Place one tray in the refrigerator. Bake the other tray for 20 minutes, or until golden brown. Let cool for about 10 minutes before enjoying. Bake the second batch of ravioli.

MIX IT UP

Hearts and Flowers and Stars, Oh My!

For experienced little bakers, upgrade from the folded ravioli shape to hearts, flowers, or stars. Stamp out two pieces of the same shape from the dough. Place a bit of filling in the center of one dough shape, and top with the second. Use fingers or a fork to press all the edges together to seal. Bake as directed.

Cheesy Ravioli Cookies

For a savory variation, skip the strawberries, sugar, and lemon zest, and add a small cube of sharp cheddar cheese in the center of each circle before folding. Sprinkle some grated Parmesan cheese on top before baking as directed.

CHEDDAR-ALMOND CRACKERS

Level 3

These nutty, cheesy soft homemade crackers are delightfully savory and make a fantastic on-the-go snack for little ones. Make a double batch—keep some in a container (for a week) and freeze the rest (up to 3 months). I create separate "stations" so each kid has a piece of dough, a rolling pin, a butter knife, and some cookie cutters. They do their thing, and only remind them to make the crackers about the same size so they'll bake evenly.

¾ cup all-purpose flour, plus more for dusting

½ cup sharp cheddar cheese

¼ cup almond flour

1 teaspoon garlic powder

¼ teaspoon baking soda

¼ teaspoon salt

4 tablespoons (½ stick) cold unsalted butter, cut into small cubes

3 tablespoons milk of your choice

2 tablespoons sea salt (optional)

1 In a food processor, combine the all-purpose flour, cheddar cheese, almond flour, garlic powder, baking soda, salt, and butter. Pulse for 1 minute to achieve a sandy texture.

2 Add the milk and pulse until it forms a soft dough.

3 Remove the dough, shape it into a ball, flatten it, and wrap in parchment paper. Refrigerate for at least 2 hours.

Active time: 30 minutes
Chill time: 2 hours
Cook time: 15 minutes, plus 10 minutes to cool

Egg-Free, Vegetarian

Makes 30 to 40 crackers

We made this recipe on:

We enjoyed:

We rate this recipe:
☆ ☆ ☆ ☆ ☆

Recipe notes:

There's more ➡

4　Preheat the oven to 350°F. Line a baking sheet with parchment paper.

5　Remove the dough from the refrigerator. Dust a flat surface with some flour and roll the dough into a ⅛-inch layer.

6　With a butter knife, cut the dough into strips and then squares, rectangles, or triangles.

7　Transfer the crackers onto the prepared baking sheet, leaving some space in between. Sprinkle with sea salt.

8　Bake for 10 to 12 minutes, or until the edges are light brown. Remove the baking sheet from the oven and let cool for 5 minutes. Taste one. If the inside is still soft, return the crackers to the oven for an extra 5 minutes. Let cool for 10 minutes and enjoy!

Make It Fun!

Instead of squares, use cookie cutters in the shape of animals, numbers, or alphabet letters. You can then use these to have fun learning!

MIX IT UP

Pumpkin Spice Crackers

Swap the all-purpose and almond flours for 1 cup of whole-wheat flour, and substitute the garlic powder with 1 tablespoon of pumpkin spice mix and add ½ cup of sugar. Sprinkle 2 tablespoons of sugar on top of the crackers instead of the sea salt. Bake as directed.

Chocolate Crackers

Swap the almond flour for ¼ cup of unsweetened cocoa powder and add ½ cup of sugar or maple syrup. Skip the cheddar and garlic, and replace the butter with coconut oil. For topping, instead of sea salt, use 1 tablespoon of orange zest. Mix the ingredients in a large bowl instead of the food processor. Bake as directed.

Active time: 30 minutes
Cook time: 40 minutes,
plus 10 minutes to cool

Dairy-Free, Gluten-Free, Vegetarian

Makes 25 to 30 small
toddler-size squares

We made this recipe on:

We enjoyed:

We rate this recipe:

☆ ☆ ☆ ☆ ☆

Recipe notes:

ZUCCHINI BROWNIES

These easy brownies are decadent, soft, creamy, airy, and definitely chocolatey! The zucchini provides nutritional value, but it also keeps the brownies nice and moist. This is a perfect party treat. Cut the brownies into small cubes and stick a colorful toothpick into each one so the kids can easily grab their chocolate bite. If you end up overbaking your brownies, don't worry. Spread some chocolate cream or whipped cream on top before cutting them.

Coconut oil or unsalted butter, for greasing

4 medium zucchini

1 cup almond butter

⅓ cup maple syrup

⅓ cup unsweetened cocoa powder

1 medium egg

¼ teaspoon salt

1 teaspoon baking soda

1 tablespoon vanilla extract

1 cup dark chocolate chips

1 Preheat the oven to 400°F and grease a 9-by-13-inch baking dish with coconut oil or butter.

2 Finely grate the zucchini (see Heads Up tip). Place the zucchini in a clean kitchen towel or paper towel and squeeze the extra water out with your hands. Place the zucchini in a large bowl.

There's more

3 To the same bowl, add the almond butter, maple syrup, cocoa powder, egg, salt, baking soda, and vanilla. Stir with a spoon until well combined. Reserve a small handful of chocolate chips, and stir the rest into the batter.

4 Transfer the batter into the baking dish and level the surface with a spoon.

5 Sprinkle the reserved chocolate chips on top.

6 Bake for 40 minutes, or until the top is shiny and dry. Let cool for about 10 minutes before cutting into squares.

MIX IT UP

Raspberry-Pecan Brownies

To add more texture, mix 1 cup of fresh raspberries and ½ cup of crushed pecans into the batter. Sprinkle a few raspberries and 2 tablespoons of crushed pecans on top along with the chocolate chips before baking as directed.

Zucchini Blondies

Substitute the unsweetened cocoa powder with almond flour, and swap the cup of chocolate chips for chopped nuts, white chocolate chips, or a mix of the two. You can also add 1 teaspoon of cinnamon. Bake as directed.

Heads Up

You can show your little helper how to use a grater safely, especially with a zucchini, which is soft and easier to grate than a hard cheese. Start by showing them the side where to grate. At first, I let them use the thin holes only; it's safer. Tell them to hold the grater with one hand to stabilize it. With the other hand, grab the zucchini from one side and start grating from top to bottom, slowly, with a bit of pressure. You can help guide the movement, showing that the zucchini needs to be angled a bit. Let them try by themselves if you think they're ready, and keep reminding, *fingers away from the grater!* Near the end, take over and finish the last small piece. Finally, let your little helper lift up the grater and *ta-da*, a mountain of fluffy zucchini!

Pies and Pastries

Don't be intimidated by the perfectly flaky pastries or the piece-of-art pies you see online. The universe of pies and pastries is full of simple, yummy, and fun recipes that you can bake and enjoy with your toddler. The Veggie Puff Pastry Tart (page 91) and the Sweet Pea and Ham Polka-Dot Quiche (page 80) are excellent art projects. Let your little ones get creative with the vegetable decoration and enjoy their edible artwork! For fun with a sweet touch, the Apple-Cinnamon Pinwheel Lollipops (page 88) will make your toddlers spin with joy.

Level 1

Active time: 20 minutes
Cook time: 55 minutes,
plus 15 minutes to cool

Nut-Free

Serves 6

We made this recipe on:

We enjoyed:

We rate this recipe:

☆ ☆ ☆ ☆ ☆

Recipe notes:

SWEET PEA AND HAM POLKA-DOT QUICHE

Quiche is always a good idea—for lunch, brunch, or even dinner. This one bursts with flavor from the toddler-friendly combo of sweet peas and savory ham. My kids call this the "polka-dot quiche" because they like to decorate the top with extra peas in a polka-dot pattern. How will your little helper decorate theirs? You can make your own crust, but I find that an easy store-bought piecrust gives me the same result, and more time to spend with my little ones decorating at the end.

1 (9-inch) store-bought frozen piecrust

1 tablespoon extra-virgin olive oil

1 scallion, finely chopped

1 cup finely diced ham

1½ cups frozen sweet peas, divided

4 medium eggs

¾ cup whole milk

1 teaspoon grainy Dijon mustard

4 ounces white cheddar cheese, cut into small cubes

1   Preheat the oven to 350°F. Remove the piecrust from the freezer and place on a baking sheet.

2   In a large skillet over medium heat, heat the olive oil for 30 seconds. Add the scallion and sauté for 1 minute, or until fragrant. Add the ham and cook for another 5 minutes until lightly golden. Add 1 cup of peas and sauté for an additional 3 minutes, or until cooked through. Transfer to a bowl and set aside to cool.

3. In a large bowl, whisk together the eggs, milk, and mustard. Add the cheese and the ham mixture, and stir until well combined.

4. Transfer the egg mixture into the piecrust, stopping about ½ inch from the top, as the filling will rise while baking. Any remaining mixture can go into mini muffin pans and bake for 15 to 18 minutes to make crustless egg muffins (fill any empty muffin holes with water.)

5. Decorate the top of the quiche with the remaining ½ cup of sweet peas.

6. Bake for 45 minutes, until golden brown. Let cool for 15 minutes before slicing and enjoying.

Heads Up

While you're sautéing, give your little helper a handful of sweet peas to play with. They can line them up, make little designs with them, count them, and even bounce, flick, and mash them with their fingers. Playing with food allows your little one to get familiar with the touch, smell, and sight of a food without the pressure of trying it, which can ease picky eating in the long run.

MIX IT UP

Spinach and Ricotta Quiche

Instead of the ham and sweet peas, sauté the scallions with 12 ounces of chopped fresh spinach. Swap the milk for ½ cup of ricotta cheese, and add ½ teaspoon of grated nutmeg and 1 teaspoon of garlic powder to the egg mixture. Bake as directed.

Gluten-Free Quiche Crust

In a large bowl, mix together 2½ cups of almond flour, 3 tablespoons of melted unsalted butter, 2 tablespoons of maple syrup, 1 medium egg, and ½ teaspoon of salt. Mix until a soft dough comes together. Transfer the dough to a 9-inch pie pan. Use your hands to press the dough into the bottom and up the sides. Proceed as directed from step 2.

Level 2

Active time: 30 minutes
Rest time: 10 minutes
Chill time: 1 hour
Cook time: 40 minutes,
plus 10 minutes to cool

Egg-Free, Vegetarian

Serves 6

We made this recipe on:

We enjoyed:

We rate this recipe:

☆ ☆ ☆ ☆ ☆

Recipe notes:

BLACKBERRY-PEACH GALETTE

My kids like the word "galette"—they say it sounds like music, and I agree! The galette is a French pastry and a close cousin of the pie, but much easier to make. Galettes are meant to be free-form and rustic, so they don't require precision or advanced pastry skills. This blackberry-peach galette has a lovely buttery and flaky pastry shell and a creamy fruity filling. If your little one has a short attention span, make the dough ahead of time, and invite them to join you at step 4.

1¼ cups all-purpose flour, plus more for dusting

¼ teaspoon sea salt

½ cup (1 stick) cold unsalted butter, cut into cubes

¼ cup ice-cold water

5 medium white or yellow peaches, pitted and sliced

¼ cup maple syrup

2 teaspoons lemon juice

1 teaspoon vanilla extract

3 tablespoons almond butter

1 cup fresh blackberries

2 tablespoons milk of your choice

2 tablespoons sugar

Vanilla ice cream, for serving (optional)

1 In a food processor on medium-low speed, process the flour, salt, butter, and cold water for a few minutes, or until the dough comes together into a compact ball.

There's more

Baker's Tip

Summer fruit is very juicy. You don't want to end up with a mushy, soggy crust because the fruit is too wet. If you see that the fruit releases too much liquid, more than 1 cup, stir 1 teaspoon of cornstarch or tapioca flour into the peaches after draining.

2 Transfer the dough to a clean, flat surface dusted with flour, and shape into a smooth ball. Wrap the dough in plastic or silicone wrap and refrigerate for at least 1 hour.

3 Preheat the oven to 400°F. Line a baking sheet with parchment paper.

4 In a bowl, stir together the peaches, maple syrup, lemon juice, and vanilla until just combined. Let it rest for 2 minutes. Stir again, and let it rest for another 5 minutes to let the peaches release their juices.

5 Drain the peaches and set aside ⅓ cup of the juice. You can offer the remaining juice to your little one.

6 Remove the dough from the refrigerator and, on a floured surface, roll it into a large circle, about 12 inches in diameter and ⅛-inch thick.

7 Using the back of a spoon, spread the almond butter in the center of the dough, leaving 1 inch around the edge. Place the peaches on top of the almond butter. Top the peaches with the reserved ⅓ cup of juice and the blackberries.

8 Gently fold the outer edges of the dough up and over some of the fruit, leaving an inner circle (about 8 inches) uncovered. Overlap the dough onto itself to create a curved edge, forming folds. Brush the milk on the edges of the crust. Sprinkle the cane sugar on top.

9 Bake for 35 to 40 minutes, or until golden brown. Let cool for 10 minutes. Enjoy with a scoop of ice cream, if desired.

MIX IT UP

Caramelized Banana and Chocolate Galette

Substitute the peaches and blackberries with 3 sliced medium, ripe bananas and 1 cup of dark chocolate chips. Place the banana slices in circles over the almond butter and sprinkle the chocolate chips on top. Bake as directed.

Cream Cheese and Summer Squash Galette

Swap the almond butter for cream cheese, and omit the ingredients from step 4. For the filling, slice 1 small zucchini and 1 small yellow summer squash, season with 2 tablespoons of olive oil and ½ teaspoon of salt and place over the cream cheese. Sprinkle grated Pecorino or Parmesan cheese on top, if desired. Replace the milk and the sugar on the crust with a drizzle of olive oil and cheese! Bake as directed.

STRAWBERRY SHORTBREAD TART

This tart has an easy shortbread crust that your little helper will love shaping and pressing into the tart pan—it's just like playing with playdough! The jam and fresh strawberry filling could not be more kid-friendly. If your toddler loves art (and you have the patience!), you can create a beautiful giant rose by slicing the strawberries vertically and overlapping the slices starting from the outside and going in a circle until you reach the center of the tart.

3 cups all-purpose flour

2½ teaspoons baking powder

½ teaspoon salt

½ cup (1 stick) unsalted butter, cut into cubes, at room temperature

½ cup sugar

1 tablespoon maple syrup

3 egg yolks

¾ cup strawberry jam

2 cups chopped fresh strawberries

1 Preheat the oven to 350°F.

2 In a large bowl, mix together the flour, baking powder, and salt until well combined. Set aside.

Level 2

Active time: 40 minutes
Cook time: 35 minutes,
plus 10 minutes to cool

Nut-Free, Vegetarian

Serves 6

We made this recipe on:

We enjoyed:

We rate this recipe:

☆ ☆ ☆ ☆ ☆

Recipe notes:

There's more ➡

Make It Fun!

Use a smaller (9-inch) tart pan and save the extra dough to make fun decorations for the top of the tart! Use three-quarters of the dough for the base and roll the remaining quarter into a ¼-inch layer. Cut it into strips and lay them in a crisscross pattern on top of the strawberries. Or, let your kid pick out a fun cookie cutter to cut out shapes from the dough and place them on top of the strawberries.

3 In another large bowl, use an electric hand mixer on medium speed to cream together the butter and sugar for 2 minutes. Add the maple syrup and egg yolks, and beat at low speed for another minute. Your little helper can take turns with you; just remind them to keep the beaters perpendicular to the bowl and close to the bottom.

4 Slowly spoon the flour mixture into the bowl with the eggs and butter, a little at a time, and stir with a wooden spoon until well combined, and the dough is smooth and silky.

5 Transfer the dough to an 11-inch tart pan. Using clean hands, spread and press the dough evenly into the bottom and up the sides of the pan.

6 Bake the crust for 10 minutes, or until lightly browned. Remove from the oven and let rest until cool enough to handle.

7 Using the back of a spoon, spread the strawberry jam on the bottom of the crust. Distribute the strawberry pieces evenly on top of the jam.

8 Return the tart to the oven and bake for an additional 20 to 22 minutes, or until the jam is bubbly and the crust is golden brown. Let cool for 10 minutes. Slice and enjoy!

MIX IT UP

Mini Strawberry Tarts

You can also use a 12-cup muffin tin to make mini tarts. Grease the muffin cups with 1 tablespoon of butter. Fill each cup with a tablespoon of dough and, using your fingers, spread the dough across the bottom and a third of the way up the cup to create a tart shell. They don't need to be prebaked. Fill each cup with a few teaspoons of strawberry jam and top with a whole strawberry, top up. Bake at 350°F for 15 to 20 minutes, until the tarts are lightly golden brown.

Chocolate Hazelnut Tart with Almonds and Blueberries

Swap the strawberry jam for ½ cup of chocolate hazelnut spread mixed with ¼ cup of warm milk to thin it out. Top with ½ cup of sliced almonds and 1½ cups of fresh blueberries. Bake as directed.

Active time: 30 minutes
Cook time: 1 hour
(30 minutes per batch),
plus 5 minutes to cool

Egg-Free, Nut-Free, Vegetarian

Makes 15 pinwheels

We made this recipe on:

We enjoyed:

We rate this recipe:

☆ ☆ ☆ ☆ ☆

Recipe notes:

APPLE-CINNAMON PINWHEEL LOLLIPOPS

What could be more fun than a pastry lollipop that smells and tastes like fall? The spiced applesauce is nice and smooth with a little lemon zest for extra zing. For more texture, you can sprinkle in some chopped pecans, almonds, or dried cranberries. Inserting wooden ice pop sticks will take some extra work, so you can skip that if you're short on time, but your little one will love being able to hold these pinwheels and bite into them!

All-purpose flour, for dusting

1 (10-by-15-inch) sheet frozen puff pastry, thawed

½ cup applesauce

1 tablespoon melted coconut oil

¼ cup sugar

Zest of ½ small lemon

½ teaspoon ground cinnamon

¼ teaspoon ground cloves

4 tablespoons whole milk

1. Preheat the oven to 400°F and line 2 baking sheets with parchment paper.

2. Unroll the puff pastry over a floured work surface. Use a rolling pin dusted with flour to gently roll over the puff pastry to smooth out any seams.

There's more

Baker's Tip

You can thaw frozen puff pastry overnight in the fridge, or simply place it on the countertop for 30 minutes. You want the pastry to be soft enough to roll, but not so soft that it's sticky and hard to work with. If that happens, stick it back in the freezer for 5 minutes. You can also store the stuffed pastry log in the freezer for 15 minutes before slicing it if it's getting too soft.

3 In a small bowl, stir together the applesauce and coconut oil and set aside. In another small bowl, mix together the sugar, lemon zest, cinnamon, and cloves. Set aside.

4 With the back of a small spoon, gently spread the applesauce mix evenly on the puff pastry, leaving a ½-inch border on all sides. Sprinkle the lemon spice mixture evenly over the applesauce.

5 Starting from the long side, slowly roll the dough up into a log. Cut the log into 1-inch rolls. Turn your knife on its side, insert it about halfway into the side of each roll, and remove it.

6 Insert a wooden ice pop stick into each knife slit, making sure the sticks are about halfway in. Place them flat on the prepared baking sheets, 2 to 3 inches apart. Brush the tops of the pinwheels with milk.

7 Bake one sheet of pops for 30 minutes until the pastry is cooked through and golden brown. Let cool for 5 minutes before enjoying. Repeat with the remaining sheet.

MIX IT UP

Spinach and Cream Cheese Pinwheels

This savory twist on the recipe is a great way to offer spinach to toddlers. Replace the spiced applesauce with ½ cup of cream cheese, 1 packed cup of baby spinach, and 2 tablespoons of milk pulsed in a food processor until smooth. Spread the mixture on the puff pastry and follow steps 5 through 8. For cheesier pinwheels, sprinkle 2 tablespoons of grated Parmesan cheese on top after brushing with milk.

Mini Pizza Lollipops

Transform the pinwheels into mini pizzas! Instead of the applesauce, lemon zest, and spices, spread 5 tablespoons of tomato paste on the puff pastry and sprinkle ½ cup of shredded mozzarella over the tomato. Follow steps 5 through 8 as directed.

VEGGIE PUFF PASTRY TART

Here a base of puff pastry and cheesy ricotta is a blank canvas to be decorated by your little helper with colorful roasted veggies. A smiley face, a bouquet of flowers, abstract art—let them have fun! Their pride of ownership will increase the chances that they enjoy their vegetables, and maybe even try a new one. Feel free to use in-season veggies—bell peppers, eggplants, or green beans in summer; broccoli, butternut squash, beets, or pumpkin in fall; carrots, cauliflower, mushrooms, or sweet potatoes in winter; and asparagus and peas in spring.

1 (10-by-15-inch) sheet frozen puff pastry, thawed

1 small green zucchini, cut into rounds

1 small yellow zucchini, cut into rounds

5 asparagus stalks, cut in 1-inch sections

8 to 10 cherry tomatoes, halved

1¼ teaspoons sea salt, divided

3 tablespoons extra-virgin olive oil

4 tablespoons ricotta cheese

4 tablespoons grated Parmesan cheese, divided

1 tablespoon all-purpose flour

4 fresh basil leaves

1   Preheat the oven to 425°F and line a large baking sheet with parchment paper. Set aside.

Level 3

Active time: 30 minutes
Cook time: 40 minutes,
plus 5 minutes to cool

Egg-Free, Nut-Free, Vegetarian

Serves 6

We made this recipe on:

We enjoyed:

We rate this recipe:
☆ ☆ ☆ ☆ ☆

Recipe notes:

There's more ➡

2 In a medium bowl, combine the green and yellow zucchini, asparagus, and tomatoes. Sprinkle 1 teaspoon of salt on top and drizzle with the olive oil. Toss them to evenly coat. Transfer the vegetables to the lined baking sheet, spacing the veggies apart. You can also use two baking sheets instead of one.

3 Roast the vegetables for 18 to 20 minutes, until tender and charred golden brown on the edges.

4 Remove the baking sheet from the oven and set aside. Reduce the temperature to 400°F.

5 In a medium bowl, mix together the ricotta, the remaining ¼ teaspoon of salt, and 2 tablespoons of Parmesan cheese. Set aside.

6 On a flat surface dusted with flour, roll out the puff pastry sheet. Using a knife, gently score the edges to create an inner square 1 inch in from the outer edge. Make sure not to cut all the way through the pastry. Scoring will allow the border to rise and get puffy once baked, like a picture frame.

7 Using the back of a tablespoon, spread the ricotta inside the inner square. Decorate the ricotta as desired with a single layer of roasted vegetables. Sprinkle the remaining 2 tablespoons of Parmesan cheese on top.

8 Bake for 20 minutes, until the pastry is puffed up, golden, and crispy. Let cool for 5 minutes, garnish with the basil leaves, and enjoy!

MIX IT UP

Peach-Mango Tart

Add ½ teaspoon of sugar to the ricotta, and spread it on the puff pastry. Omit the vegetables from step 2. Cut one peach and half a mango in slices. Add the mango and peach slices on top of the ricotta, lightly overlapping. Sprinkle another ½ teaspoon of sugar on top. Bake as directed.

Pesto-Tomato Tart

For a stronger flavor, swap the ricotta base for 4 tablespoons of basil pesto and top it with 1 cup of halved cherry tomatoes or a medium heirloom tomato cut in ½-inch slices. For even more flavor, you can use 2 tablespoons of olive tapenade as a base if your little ones appreciate olives. To mellow out the olives, mix it with 2 tablespoons of ricotta before spreading it on. Bake as directed.

measurement conversions

Oven Temperatures	
Fahrenheit (F)	**Celsius (C) (approx.)**
250°F	120°C
300°F	150°C
325°F	165°C
350°F	180°C
375°F	190°C
400°F	200°C
425°F	220°C
450°F	230°C

Volume Equivalents (Liquid)		
Standard	**US Standard (oz.)**	**Metric (approx.)**
2 tablespoons	1 fl. oz.	30 mL
¼ cup	2 fl. oz.	60 mL
½ cup	4 fl. oz.	120 mL
1 cup	8 fl. oz.	240 mL
1½ cups	12 fl. oz.	355 mL
2 cups or 1 pint	16 fl. oz.	475 mL
4 cups or 1 quart	32 fl. oz.	1 L
1 gallon	128 fl. oz.	4 L

Weight Equivalents	
Standard	**Metric (approx.)**
½ ounce	15 g
1 ounce	30 g
2 ounces	60 g
4 ounces	115 g
8 ounces	225 g
12 ounces	340 g
16 ounces or 1 pound	455 g

Volume Equivalents (Dry)	
Standard	**Metric (approx.)**
⅛ teaspoon	0.5 mL
¼ teaspoon	1 mL
½ teaspoon	2 mL
¾ teaspoon	4 mL
1 teaspoon	5 mL
1 tablespoon	15 mL
¼ cup	59 mL
⅓ cup	79 mL
½ cup	118 mL
⅔ cup	156 mL
¾ cup	177 mL
1 cup	235 mL
2 cups or 1 pint	475 mL
3 cups	700 mL
4 cups or 1 quart	1 L

resources

Amazon.com or **Michaels.com** If you can't find baking items at your local store, cookie cutters, colored spatulas, small rolling pins, pans, and whisks are easily found here.

BusyToddler.com Susie is a mom of three, a former teacher, an early childhood education advocate, and the most creative parent you can imagine. Keeping a toddler's body and mind busy and entertained is her magic skill.

EllynSatterInstitute.org Ellyn Satter is an expert and author on feeding infants and kids. She devoted her career to transforming family meals into joyful, healthful, struggle-free events.

Etsy.com My favorite place for a personalized gift, and it supports small businesses. Your little helper will be so excited to receive an apron with their name on it, or a set of mini spoons and spatulas or mini measuring cups that are easy to hold.

HappyKidsKitchen.com Heather is the author of the first book of this series, "Little Helpers Toddler Cookbook," and an amazing cooking teacher for kids. Her two kids are her first students. Making food fun, appealing, and tasty is an art she excels in.

KidsEatInColor.com Jennifer is a friend, mom, and registered dietitian who offers valuable insights for parents looking to get their picky kids to eat veggies. With empathy and sensitivity, Jennifer combines the dietary benefits of healthy eating with practical suggestions on how to end food battles and create good food habits.

SolidStarts.com Jenny is the beautiful soul, friend, and mom of three behind the best First Foods database, which is currently available on her website. Solid Starts is the place to go and check if a specific food is appropriate for little ones in terms of nutrition and age development. It also offers useful tips and advice on starting solids and the toddler diet.

YourKidsTable.com Alisha is a friend, a mom to three boys, a licensed pediatric occupational therapist with over 14 years of experience, and an expert in feeding and sensory play. Her website is a continual source of information about picky eating, feeding, and sensory activities.

YummyToddlerFood.com Amy is not only "the toddler guru" but also has a powerful, reassuring way of explaining things. A mom of three, a recipe developer, and an author, she shares yummy, toddler-friendly recipes and many tips on feeding and toddler life in general.

BOOKS

For Adults

Busy Toddler's Guide to Actual Parenting: From Their First "No" to Their First Day of School (and Everything In Between) by Susie Allison. This book is a breath of fresh air. With her humor and engaging personality, Susie helps parents find their footing, shift their perspective on childhood, and laugh at the twists and turns of parenting that we all face.

Fearless Feeding: How to Raise Healthy Eaters from High Chair to High School by Jill Castle and Maryann Jacobsen. This comprehensive book explains how eating relates to a child's overall development, how to make balanced food choices (and help children make them, too), and how to end feeding struggles forever.

Helping Your Child with Extreme Picky Eating: A Step-by-Step Guide for Overcoming Selective Eating, Food Aversion, and Feeding Disorders by Katja Rowell and Jenny McGlothlin. In this book, a family doctor specializing in childhood feeding joins forces with a speech pathologist to help you support your child's nutrition, healthy growth, and end mealtime anxiety (for your child *and* you) once and for all.

Little Helpers Toddler Cookbook: Healthy, Kid-Friendly Recipes to Cook Together by Heather Wish Staller. The first book of the Little Helpers series. Many healthy yummy-in-your-tummy recipes that you can make with your kids are featured in this book.

Raising a Healthy, Happy Eater: A Parent's Handbook: A Stage-by-Stage Guide to Setting Your Child on the Path to Adventurous Eating by Nimali Fernando and Melanie Potock. Helpful insights and advice on how to expand your family's food horizons, avoid the picky eater trap, identify special feeding needs, and put joy back into mealtimes.

The Science of Mom: A Research-Based Guide to Your Baby's First Year by Alice Callahan. This friendly guide through the science of infancy explains how non-scientist mothers can learn the difference between hype and evidence.

For Kids

Busy Little Hands: Food Play! Activities for Preschoolers by Amy Palanjian. Colorful, photo-driven recipes that encourage kids to discover and expand their tastes, and experience the joy and pride that come from making the foods they eat with their own hands.

Eating the Alphabet by Lois Ehlert. While teaching upper- and lowercase letters to preschoolers, the book introduces fruits and vegetables from around the world. A glossary at the end provides interesting facts about each food.

Eat Your Colors by Amanda Miller. An engaging toddler book about food and colors from the Rookie Toddler series.

The Good Egg by Jory John. A funny and charming story that reminds us of the importance of balance, self-care, and accepting those we love (even if they are sometimes a bit rotten).

Hello, Arnie! An Arnie the Doughnut Story by Laurie Keller. One of the fun adventures of Arnie the Doughnut and his bakery friends.

If You Give a Mouse a Cookie by Laura Numeroff. A lovely cookie-inspired book for story time or beginning readers.

Marigold Bakes a Cake by Mike Malbrough. A lovely baking story from the Marigold cat series that you can read to your toddler before or after baking together.

Pancakes with Grandma by Kathryn Smith. A lovely lift-the-flap book. Join Grandma Bunny and Little Bunny as they make pancakes together.

Stir Crack Whisk Bake: A Little Book about Little Cakes by America's Test Kitchen. Let your little one experience the magic of baking cupcakes from the pages of this lovely book.

Super Foods for Super Kids Cookbook: 50 Delicious (and Secretly Healthy) Recipes Kids Will Love to Make by Noelle Martin. This cookbook has cool kitchen tutorials that teach children how to read a recipe, talk like a chef, and safely use the tools needed to sizzle, chop, and simmer their favorite foods. It features easy-to-read instructions and 50 recipes for yummy treats, snacks, and meals.

recipe level index

index

acknowledgments

A huge thank-you to the amazing Callisto Publishing team for finding me, convincing me, and making me sit down and write this book while an unprecedented pandemic was freezing the world. Baking recipes with my kids, doing research, and writing about the pleasures and challenges of cooking with toddlers was such a source of relaxation and self-care. It reminded me that we need to cherish every single moment with our loved ones, and made me look at the lockdown through different eyes.

My adventure in the baby and toddler food world would never have started without the constant encouragement, support, and love of my hubby, Albert. Thank you for being my most passionate and honest critic, my first thumbs-up for every video I post, and loving me just the way I am.

To Alex and Luca: You are my inspiration, my picky testers, and the reason I wake up every morning with a smile. Love you x 3000.

To Mamma. *Scrivo in Italiano così non dovrai chiedere la traduzione. Grazie per esserci sempre, grazie per essere la mia colonna, grazie per essere la nonna migliore che Alex e Luca potrebbero desiderare.*

A huge virtual hug to my lovely and talented editor, Ada, for her always-positive and constructive feedback and her guidance and help in every step.

And last, but not least at all, a huge XOXO to all the readers, followers, and subscribers out there who have been following *BuonaPappa* since the beginning as well as the ones who just started yesterday. This book is for you. Your continued support and love make me keep going with passion and joy in every recipe I share.

about the author

Barbara Lamperti is the recipe developer, photographer, and video creator behind the blog and YouTube channel *BuonaPappa*, where she shares her passion for healthy food starting from the very first baby spoon. Author of the *Fuss-Free Toddler Cookbook*, Barbara is devoted to sharing nourishing recipes using fresh, local, and seasonal ingredients to raise healthy babies, toddlers, and children. Her happy place is the farmers' market, where she can be found every Sunday morning with her kids. Originally from Italy, Barbara lives with her husband and their two boys in Los Angeles.

For more recipe inspirations and videos, find her online at:

BuonaPappa.net

YouTube.com/user/buonapappa

Instagram.com/buonapappa

Printed in the USA
CPSIA information can be obtained
at www.ICGtesting.com
LVHW060410120124
768705LV00003B/26